ANGER MANAGEMENT WORKBOOK FOR MEN

A Definitive Beginner's Guide to Take Control of Your Anger and Master Your Emotions, How To Calm Down, Managing your Emotions, Criticism, and Increased Emotional Intelligence

Copyright © 2022 William Richards All rights reserved.

No part of this guide may be reproduced in any form without permission in writing from the publisher except in the case of brief quotations embodied in critical articles or reviews.

Legal & Disclaimer

The information contained in this book and its contents is not designed to replace or take the place of any form of medical or professional advice; and is not meant to replace the need for independent medical, financial, legal or other professional advice or services, as may be required. The content and information in this book have been provided for educational and entertainment purposes only.

The content and information contained in this book has been compiled from sources deemed reliable, and it is accurate to the best of the Author's knowledge, information and belief. However, the Author cannot guarantee its accuracy and validity and cannot be held liable for any errors and/or omissions. Further, changes are periodically made to this book as and when needed. Where appropriate and/or necessary, you must consult a professional (including but not limited to your doctor, attorney, financial advisor or such other professional advisor) before using any of the suggested remedies, techniques, or information in this book.

Upon using the contents and information contained in this book, you agree to hold harmless the Author from and against any damages, costs, and expenses, including any legal fees potentially resulting from the application of any of the information provided by this book. This disclaimer applies to any loss, damages or injury caused by the use and application, whether directly or indirectly, of any advice or information presented, whether for breach of contract, tort, negligence, personal injury, criminal intent, or under any other cause of action.

You agree to accept all risks of using the information presented inside this book.

You agree that by continuing to read this book, where appropriate and/or necessary, you shall consult a professional (including but not limited to your doctor, attorney, or financial advisor or such other advisor as needed) before using any of the suggested remedies, techniques, or information in this book.

TABLE OF CONTENTS

Table of Contents _____ 3

Introduction _____ 6

Chapter 1: The 101 Guide Through Anger Management _____ 13

Chapter 2: Reasons and Triggers for Anger Outbursts in people _____ 30

Chapter 3: Managing your Emotions _____ 37

Chapter 4: Basic Lessons of Anger Management _____ 53

Chapter 5: Practical Aspects of Anger Management _____ 61

Chapter 6: Handling Facts and Taking The suppression to the next level _____ 69

Chapter 7: Shifting Focus to manage anger even better _____ 74

Chapter 8: Solving things one at a time _____ 80

Chapter 9: Discussion on Anger Triggers _____ 84

Chapter 10: Managing Criticism _____ 92

Chapter 11: Criticism (more) _____ 97

Chapter 12: Mind game _____ 101

Chapter 13: Extras _____ 108

Conclusion _____ 111

Anger management workbook for men

Anger management workbook for men

INTRODUCTION

Emotions and feelings are the only two things that makes us as a totally different living creature in this world. if you are talking about how exactly the entire world and all the life existing in it are behaving, these two things are the only things that sets us apart from the animals.

Emotion doesn't always mean that you need to feel weak or be in love with someone. Just as being love with someone is a specific type of emotion, so are all the other things that we don't usually like in a personality. And within the list of the emotions that we don't actually admire too much, are the negative emotions or the dark side of human personality. You might have a question regarding what are these dark emotions? if you think about jealousy or anger or anxiety or any other type of emotion that does not give you a good feeling, is basically a negative emotion. this book is all about how you can manage one of the worst enemy of mankind. It is definitely not terrorism, erase not crime. The worst enemy ever known to mankind is the anger of themselves.

Let me give you a little perspective about what anger is truly capable of. Anger is basically the very root or the very base of all the wrong doings ever done by a human. Doesn't matter what type of guy you are or even what type of environment that you are living in, if you have a lot of anger in your personality that is definitely not going to be good for you at all.

I know this for a fact because, if you think about a person who has a lot of anger Management related issues. You can easily think about a lot of related problems that

Anger management workbook for men

this guys going to have. I mean, you just name it. Anything that you can imagine from simple negative emotions such as anxiety and jealousy towards some harsh adverse of anger such as physical assault or even verbal abuse or even sometimes causing the person himself to turn out really furious criminal.

This book is designed and also researched and written in such a manner that you don't only get the ways are the tips and tricks about how to solve your anger Management related issues. rather than doing just the tips and tricks parts like most of the other content available on the internet, I tried my best to actually helped my readers to understand the problem from its base and take the best action to get rid of it.

If you think about it like this, you can easily just search on Google for tips and tricks about how to get rid of anger. you will get a lot of articles and literally thousands of them just telling you how you can get rid of anger related issues from doing meditation or thinking about something with a different perspective and so on. All these information are basically available just at a click of your mouse. So, If you can get literally thousands of article related to how to get rid of your anger, then why the earth has so much hatred and so much violence in eight right now? People would have just simply read those articles and get free from their anger right?

The fact is, learning information only helps in terms of knowing that there is a way. But how to utilize that way totally depends on how actually you are capable of understanding the problem. Let me give you a little bit of clarification right here. Imagine that, you have a car for yourself. The piece of element that basically powers of the car to go forward and take you to the places that you need to be is the engine. Which means that we can say that

Anger management workbook for men

engine is the most important part of a vehicle. But how will you make sure that you are going in just the direction that you want to go. That my friend, would be the steering wheel. In this case that I am talking about, gathering information is without any reasonable doubt, the most important part of solving a problem. But that is not all of it. You need a proper power to actually use the information that you have inside your head, or all of those information are not going to be useful to you at all.

Before I was starting this book I want to tell you something about solving problems. You might be able to find a lot of articles or even a lot of books at your local market or even on amazon.com or just by a simple Google search. Those articles or those books are going to be regarding how you can change your life in simple 10 steps, or even how you can change your life in just 30 days, or 7 days or in 24 hours or just by simply following these hundred steps etc.

If those were really helpful then people would have been suffering from such problems and more in this world. The one thing that people lack to understand is that they need a proper understanding of the entire problem so that they can process that information in order to solve the problem.

And that is exactly what I tried to teach or to explain towards my reader. I want to tell you that don't just try to understand and learn more and more information about how you can actually solve the problem. Before learning about just how to and what to, learn about the problem itself. Learn about the causes of it. Learn about the reason for its existence. You might have seen a lot of books about mastering specific skills for self development or self help or even sometimes achieving a

Anger management workbook for men

certain skill set. You don't need to be a professional or a master in order to execute a certain task with procession.

What you actually need, tips to understand the task first before trying to doing it and trying to learn about how to do it. You might have a thought in your head that all of these efforts that you will be giving is basically a waste of time rather than you should just learn about how to solve the problem first. Your thinking is obviously reasonable and rational. But that is not how you are going to be achieving 100% precession and also efficiency in terms of the efforts that you are given to a process.

Before telling you the next thing that I was about to, let me give you a little bit of hand of who I am and what I do and why I am speaking to you about all of these. I am William Richards. I am basically a sociological researcher. Apart from the corporate job that I have, there is one hobby that I admire the most in myself. That is why I usually spend a lot of my free time in doing research and also I do a lot of travelling to complete those research regarding human psychology and self help. Now, let's talk about the part which I left. If you have read any other book that I have done in the past, you already know what I am going to say. If you haven't then allow me to explain.

Every problem and the entire process of its solution is not like a table. It is more like a complete cycle. If you take off one leg from a table it might still be able to balance if you put a counter weight on the part which it has legs. but if you take a small element away from a complete cycle then the entire process will simply fall down. And solving a problem is exactly like a cycle not like a table. If you truly want to solve a problem and also be free from some issues that you have in your personal life, then you need to understand the problem first before trying to achieve the solution.

Anger management workbook for men

Tell me one thing. if you do not understand the problem with a proper depth research and information, then how are you going to be so sure that you actually have achieved the solution that you desire? How are you going to be so sure that the solution that you have come up with is actually good and sustainable? That is exactly why you need to understand about the problem first not the solutions.

If you have purchased this book from amazon.com, you might have noticed a couple of things in the website while you're doing the search. There are a lot of books that just tell you 100 ways to get rid of anger. Even 30 days workbook to get rid of your anger management issues. Search type of attractive titles and attractive and well detailed information about the book is of course commendable without any reason. But the thing is, if you truly want to achieve that success of solving the problem of anger in your personality, I know that this book is going to be boring but I am still telling you that give this a proper read and by the end of it you will have a much better understanding about what the problem is and how you can get rid of it.

I could have just told you that you would have 100% accuracy of solving a problem and you would simply get rid of your problem within a short amount of time with guarantee. But that is not how I work. I acknowledge this that how I worked or how I don't doesn't actually have to do anything with solving the problem. But the reality is that, that is also not how the way it should be done if you really want to achieve the success. And of course, when we are talking about such type of sensitive subject such as anger Management, you need nothing but the best. And that, is exactly why I am here. I will not promise you that you will be getting rid of

Anger management workbook for men

your anger management problem just like that. I am promising to you right now that, I will make you capable of getting rid of the problem. I will give you the tools, the knowledge, the guidance. How you are going to be walking on the path is totally up to you.

At this point, I do realize that I might be sounding a little bit pessimist. But if you continue on with the first couple of chapters you will easily understand what I am trying to say and how you can get a lot of benefits from the knowledge that I am about to share with you in this book.

You might have a certain feeling inside your head that all of these processes and learning and these small talks are not going to be helpful and these are all nothing but a proper waste of time. But think this, if you are already suffering with anger related issues, you might have already lost a lot of your happy times from your life. What's the damage to just give it a small that will try once again?

I am not here in front of you with this book just to make you understand about how you can make your life like heaven. I am here, in front of you through this book, as a person that understands. A person that understands the type of problem that you are going through. A person that understands that you need someone or something that will understand just in the way that you are and not just force some different ways about a dumb solution.

Before actually starting with the first chapter I want to say another thing to you. The first couple of chapters regarding the introduction and understanding about anger and how it can be managed it might seem a little bit boring. And there is absolutely nothing that I can sugar-coat.

Anger management workbook for men

But I will not obviously lie to you. What I truly want, is to just tell you some stories and some things here and there. Not because of am just wasting your time and trying to sell my book and make a lot of money out of it. Is because I just want to share the knowledge.

This was just some foreword of this book. If you still somehow have not lost the attraction to this book, know this. the effort that you are still giving in reading this book besides of the boring introduction that I have just completed, already proves that you are willing to solve the problem and be a better person. You can say that this is may be 90% of the entire thing done.

Willing to solve a problem and develop yourself is something that most of the population really lack of. But if you are always willing to solve the problem and if you are actually willing to commit yourself to the process of learning and understanding, then don't worry. You will get through this just find.

Anger management workbook for men

CHAPTER 1: THE 101 GUIDE THROUGH ANGER MANAGEMENT

What is anger Management

Just like I have told you in the beginning, anger is one of the worst enemy ever known to mankind. And if you really want to get rid of this enemy and fight back then you need the proper knowledge and also the proper management of the entire problem along with the understanding.

Let's start with the basics first without wasting any more time.

If you want a formal introduction for a formal definition to this term, anger management is basically a simple process of understanding and recognizing the symptoms that you are becoming angry. And taking the proper action to calm yourself down and also dealing with the specific situation in a much efficient and productive manner.

If you want a more scientific or medical type of definition for this term then I can tell you that, anger Management is simply a psychological therapy program for those who have anger related outbursts and similar issues and giving them a proper structure to follow so that they can provide proper prevention and also the control for their anger. You can also say that it is basically the process of deploying the anger inside a personality with successful results. Anger might be a result of frequent amount of frustration or even the sensation or feeling of being blocked or thrown away from something that you

Anger management workbook for men

desire the most or which is really important to your emotions. anger is not necessarily always the result of frustration or even the rejection from a certain thing. Anger can be also a result for a response on the differences aside from a personality due to some certain fear of feelings or even some type of in security and vulnerability. Programs related to anger Management training usually considered as anchor to be a specific amount of motivation that has been caused by any type of identifiable cause of action which obviously has the capability of being analyzed on a logical basis.

I understand that the last part that I just told you might seem a little bit complicated and way too much scientific for a normal person to understand. Let me put down a simple explanation and example for you.

Anger is a specific type of negative emotion inside a personality that is usually caused by some salt of deprivation. This deprivation can be from such type of object that a person feels that he deserves to achieve that. Even, anger can be a result for a defense mechanism in terms of feeling insecure in a certain situation.

But the peculiar thing is, despite of being for a certain and very validated reason, ankle has never been considered anything good for a personality. Rather than it has been more identified and recognized as one of the bad sides of a personality that can cause a lot of other trouble such as anxiety or the feeling of being insecure or sometimes lack of confidence. But that is not the worst part about anger. The worst thing that anger can make a person do is really an emergency and beyond anyone's thoughts. Anger is capable of turning a simple and quite humble person into someone really criminal and really negative towards the society and the person that are usually around him. If you imagine your mind or your

Anger management workbook for men

personality or even your soul as something that is sacred and clean. In that case, anger is the filthiest and the dirtiest thing that can make that sacred soul or that sacred existence dark.

Now let's learn some other basic information about anger Management. The straightforward goal of a proper anger Management session or a proper exercise or working schedule for anger management is to bring proper control and also regulate the amount of anger in a personality in such a way that, it does not result in any sort of problems whether on a personal basis or even on a social basis.

Anger is basically an active type of emotion that causes a person to respond with outburst reactions.

People who are more likely to enter into a angry situation or angry state of mind, are suffering from step of issues more likely because both of the parties of instigator and instigated are lacking proper amount of interpersonal and also skills related to social communications and failure to maintain proper amount of self-control. Research conducted on such type of effect and also self regulation has been showing us that the anger related issues are occurring more likely because the negative state of emotional condition inside a personality of a lot of impairment with impulse control. anger Management related professional sessions and formal training courses more likely train their subjects to provide proper respond towards something that is making them angry in such a manner that they are able to avoid that certain impulsive reaction and also that emotion in a certain time.

if you are a person that is interested in to literature then you might have noticed that several works from popular writers, even those which are written at

Anger management workbook for men

least a couple of hundred years ago, have been showing a certain amount of anger development in personality and how it has been able to disable the common and obvious reactions of a person along with the perspective towards a certain situation.

Let me give you a circumstance imagine. Let's assume that you are a person that has a large number of friends in your circle along with a healthy relationship with all the family members. Despite of being really close to your friends and family is not always necessary that you will be sharing every single element or every single details of your personal life with them. you might think that this is not good and this is just a symbol of not having a healthy relationship with those you love. But the truth is, there are some certain things that we cannot just share with anyone. I mean, just imagine, would you just go around and tell everyone what happened to you the entire day? Doesn't it seem way too much lame? Of course it is. This is something that no one can avoid that a person has a lot of things that he or she keeps to himself or herself due to some personal reasons. And obviously I am not telling you to just go around and share everything with everyone that you love. I am just telling you how it all starts. When you are having such type of stressful moments or events in your life and obviously those events are not known by those who are around you, it is obvious that they are going to be giving out their usual responses towards your existence that they usually do. But when you are in a stressed situation or even really anxious about something, that simple joyful hello can even trigger your anger if you are stressed and frustrated enough. And in that situation, lashing out with impulsive reaction is much common and sometimes obvious. And anger Management actually helps you with controlling such type of obvious and impulsive reactions and helps you a lot in terms of

Anger management workbook for men

keeping your anxiety in a proper control and also keeping the proper and healthy relationship with those around you.

Now the we have discussed a lot about what anger Management really is, let's talk about why anger Management and such type of effort to get rid of anger is important.

Importance of anger Management

Anger is a type of emotion that every single human being experiences a lot in their lifetime. Whatever the cause or however the nature of the person may be, anger should never be allowed to grow out in such a manner that is out of control and it is often drawn towards escalating into violent reaction and also ruining a lot of healthy relationships. If you are a person that has a lot of struggling times with dealing with your emotion of anger then you should probably seek a proper assistance for getting your anger management into a proper control and also you need to be trying by yourself.

And you need to act fast before it's too late.

A lot of people in the modern society are struggling with a certain amount of feeling that if the anger that they have inside them, starts taking control of them, they are not going to be able to maintain the relationship that they have with the people that around them. the most unfortunate part about this entire situation is that anger basically leaves a person psychologically and also socially injured while facing sometimes criminal charges. Sometimes even with a lot of laws regarding relationships. When anger is taking over

Anger management workbook for men

your life it will slowly starts to feel your motive which can easily leave you in a tendency to seek revenge even for the smallest offence done against you that doesn't even count as an offence. the sensation of the emotion of anger is capable of making you feel harm where you are actually not and the actual damages that has been done is so small that is easily ignorable. the worst score about having anger is that it does not allow you to think logically rather than it forces you to lash out with impulsive reaction and also sometimes it makes you a lot violent. Even the slightest in balance of the situation in front of you which could have been dealt with just a little couple of words, anger would force you to lash out violently. And I must say that in such type of situations, you will feel a lot of difficulty in terms of talking yourself down from a state of anger and it is going to be even harder if you don't have the right knowledge and the tools to do so.

When I am saying that anger creates a lot of difficulties in terms of maintaining healthy relationships, I am not only referring towards relationship that are based out of romantic affection. Anger is capable of ruining and also living a severe and irremovable impact of your relationship with friends or even family.

If you are just thinking about someone who you really know on a close basis has been struggling with a lot of issues related to his or her anger Management in the past life, you can get a lot of information from them regarding how they have been maintaining their anger issues. We constantly hear from different type of therapy and also counselling sessions that we need to surround ourselves with such type of personalities that are happy and positive. And we hear this all the time whether directly from a counselling session or even on the television advertisement or any other informative content

Anger management workbook for men

related to psychological health. We hear this literally everywhere whenever there is discussion regarding to psychological or mental health. This is all happening for a certain reason. a positive personality doesn't necessarily mean that he or she needs to accept every wrong things that you have been doing. a positive personality basically means that doesn't matter what type of mistake you are doing he or she will encourage you to do the right thing not just pointing out mistakes and tell you that how much failure that you have pain in your life.

The worst part about anger is that sometimes it creates an illusion in front of you that you are receiving the attention that you should be. Just like I said in a previous part of this book, anger can be a serious reason out of some sort of insecurity or some sort of deprivation. More than 60% or 70% of cases it has been proven that such type of insecurity are raising from issues related to not getting proper attention for a person that he truly deserves. The problem regarding such type of situation is that, whenever due to your insecurities you are giving out impulsive reactions it is going to cause a lot of attention to move towards you. And in that situation, your subconscious mind will slowly tell you that the reaction that you just gave has been capable of giving you the attention that you truly deserve and you want. And just because of that, your subconscious mind will force your actions to be just in the similar pattern from now on. Which basically means that you are going to be a grumpy and angry person for the rest of your life if you are not careful about it.

If something is giving you the result that you want and that way is not the correct way, doesn't matter how many benefits is has been giving you, you need to avoid it at all costs. Anger is a serious symptom and it can

Anger management workbook for men

be also described as a symptom related to a variety of mental health related issues. What's the positive side about this entire down situation is that anger Management and the issues related to anger is a certain type of situation that can be easily worked out and manage in a proper way. I do realise that there are a lot of therapy sessions and psychological health related doctors who will prescribe a lot of nerve relaxing medicines to calm yourself down. I am not telling you that all of those medicine are basically useless and you should not take them ever. But whenever you are taking them you need to keep in your mind that doesn't matter how much benefit it has been giving you, you cannot be dependable entirely on some medications. I will not be discussing a lot about medications and is it either good or bad for you in this chapter. There will be a totally separate and detailed discussion on this topic in a later chapter that you might have already seen in the index of this book. Now let's get back to the point that I was discussing.

Anger basically forces you into working in a manner that is not good either for you or even for the person that is in front of you. And the exercises are the methods that you need to approach in order to get your anger issues properly managed works in such type of manner that forces you to find out the root or the very base cause of your reactions. Understanding the basement of your problem actually helps you in order to get a clear vision about what the problem really is and what type of approach is going to be best for you. psychological health or mental health related issues can never be judged by the same pattern in different person. Which basically means that, doesn't matter what type of therapy or what type of doctor you are saying to get rid of your anger related issues, it is you, who needs to understand the best about

Anger management workbook for men

the problem and come up with an idea about how to approach it and get rid of it.

Anger is such type of a characteristic insert a personality that has the capability of making people think negatively about you. Normally how people are thinking about you but also anger has capability to impair your entire capability of judgement and also hijack you from your healthy relationships and your healthy life. if you are a person that obviously does not want this type of situation happening in your life, you need to understand the subject matter what I have been discussing with you.

As I have told you in the past, anger Management is a state of issue that you really need to get to the root. And to understand the problem related to anger Management and such type of issues arising out of it, the next part of this book is just for you.

Let's start with some of the basic myths that are found in our society regarding anger. There are a lot of people and also a lot of informative content that will tell you that it is good to control and suppress your anger.

before describing the last sentence let's talk about some certain aspects about this entire situation. Imagine you have been surprising your anger and not letting out your emotions when you are actually feeling it. What do you think is going to happen? If you have thought that you are going to be facing a certain situation where that entire amount of stored anger inside your mind is going to just wash out over the person that is in front of you due to some really small mistake, you are absolutely right.

Suppressing or holding onto your anger is not something that you would really want to do. It was just act

Anger management workbook for men

like a pressure cooker on a burning stove. You will just hold on to those anger inside you for a certain amount of time and also when the time comes you will be lashing every single one of them out from you in such a manner that you will seem nothing but a maniac and also and animal inside the mind of the other person.

Is this something you truly want? The entire purpose of anger management is not to make you capable of holding onto your anger and suppressing it inside your mind. That will only create more and more stress and frustration inside you. The whole purpose of anger Management and such type of exercises and practices is to make you capable of thinking about some certain things in a totally different manner so that it does not create any sorts of emotion related to anger inside your psychological state.

People are more likely to think that the entire process of anger management is all about learning how you can suppress your anger inside you and not letting it out in front of other people. But if you are suppressing your anger or never being angry is a symptom of extreme and also and healthy type of psychological state inside your subconscious mind. If anger is suppressed and stored inside your mind then it has a really risky element and potential to it. When it finds even the smallest crack in your personality to come out then it is going to be coming out so loud and so explosively, you will be quite shocked by yourself.

Anger Management basically targets and helps you in order to spot the exact reason and the nature of the anger and then predict it coming and learning to face it in such a way that will provide you productive outcomes for yourself and also for those who are around you.

Anger management workbook for men

If I keep on talking about why and how anger management is important and necessary for your life that I can go on pages after pages all day long. Just let's come to the base line about what I have been talking so far.

anger Management is not necessary just because of you want to get rid of how you have been reacting towards people. Forget about other people. Forget about anyone else existing in this entire world. Just think about yourself. If you are such a person that has been suffering a lot with anger related issues then you might have noticed a major thing about such type of impulsive reactions. Whenever you are getting angry and your rearing of screaming and shouting at someone, at some point after the impressive situation you automatically calm down. Have you ever realized that when your anger is gone in that moment, the next thing that comes in your mind is extreme level of guilt. Even if the anger is not harmful for you then the aftermath of angry situation is going to slowly kill you from the inside. And that is really the worst part about this India situation.

Getting rid of your anger related issues does not always mean that you are doing it for how others are feeling about you. It's mostly important and necessary for you to get rid of your own bad conscience and be on the good side of your own mind.

Let's discuss about a little bit on how anger does all the harm inside your personality and also how it affects your life in the worst way possible.

Anger management workbook for men

Why anger is bad for you

By this part of this book you might have already understood a lot about how and why anger is bad for a person's life. But, like all the other good things, it doesn't cause any harm to put a little bit more in faces and also a little bit more discussion regarding how you can make your life better than before.

Without any reasonable doubt it is proven that anger is bad for your health condition. Doesn't matter if you are talking about mental health or even physical health. Anger is such type of a negative trait that has compatibility of leaving a significant effect on to your overall existence. According to several research, just after a person has faced any type of outburst of anchor there has been found significant amount of risk of heart attack within the next 2 hours.

In the modern world from just going towards the school to getting around to the supermarket it is obvious that everywhere and almost everyone is really on a short time fuse. The reason is that there are so many different activities and so many different processes in our regular life to be maintained in a single amount of time. As time goes by, people are more likely to be having much more complicated times and complicated schedules to maintain in their daily routine. Which that complicated schedule it is very much possible that a normal person is going to be quite frustrated and also stressed out at a certain time. The world is not going anywhere from being the way that it is already. It is us, who needs to adopt and adapt new methods and tactics in our daily life and also in our

Anger management workbook for men

thinking pattern so that we are one step ahead of this stressful and frustrating life and also at the same time we are able to manage all of the stresses with proper efficiency so that we are getting the best out of the efforts that we are giving in. When we are getting angry or annoyed at something or someone, our body starts undergoing a response pattern which is known as fight or flight. We experience with increased amount of hormone into our blood stream which basically puts our body into a condition of arousal and also dampens our immune system in terms of keeping our mind calm down. If we are staying angry for a longer period of time it is very much possible that the increased amount of adrenaline and the rush of blood that is going to be running through our veins are going to be causing a significant amount of damage into our blood flow system and also our straight thinking compatibility. Doesn't matter what type of aspect of your point of view you are looking at. Anger has the capability and obviously does a significant amount of damage in every single aspect of our life. Doesn't matter if it is physical or psychological or event social.

Under all circumstances, anger has been giving us and will be giving us nothing but bad and negative things to experience.

A properly managed state of anger can usually be a set of useful emotions that has the capability to motivate a person towards making positive changes in his or her life. But the problem is that, at the same, anger is such an emotion with a lot of power that if it has not been handled properly, it will bring nothing but this truck 2 results for the person who is suffering with the condition along with physical fights sometimes abuse, assault and also self harm.

Anger management workbook for men

In this chapter I will be discussing about several stages of damage that you can have due to anger related issues.

I have already discussed about the fight or flight type of response that your body starts to give whenever you are in an angry stage. There are also several other common and long-lasting problems that a person is going to be facing if he or she has been exposed to longer periods of anger.

Such type of problem can be as simple as a constant headache towards as serious as a stroke or even a heart attack. If we somehow disregard all of the physical issues that we are going to be facing due to anger, even then, our entire existence and the entire balance of life is going to be at risk of getting jeopardized due to this small little thing in our personality.

If you are getting mad all the time at everything and at every single in balance in front of you, you are more likely to be finding yourself in such a state that you have been falling sick more often in comparison with others. A study conducted by Harvard University scientists has shown us that healthy people and joyful people have a much less risk of getting prone towards small sickness such as seasonal fever or even headache and nausea or anxiety and several other common diseases. This thing has been underestimated and also ignored by maybe millions of people All around The world that being happy has nothing to do with a proper health condition. People are more likely to think that if you maintain yourself right then you will be right. But that is not obviously the whole truth. The emotions that we feel it doesn't matter if it is happiness or sadness or even anger triggers a specific set of hormones to grow and flow through our blood stream. Which basically means that whenever we are facing a

Anger management workbook for men

specific emotion inside our brain we are getting a overdose of a specific hormone inside our blood stream. And the type of hormone that anger usually release into our blood stream is compatible of weakening our immune system. So if we really want to make ourselves better in terms of not only how we are thinking or how we are living in a mental state, but also at the same time we want to keep our physical existence as strong as our mental existence. Getting rid of anger and also trying to think and mastering the art of changing your perspective towards something that it no longer has the capability to make you mad, is may be the most important part that you should learn in your practical life.

Just like I said in a previous part of this chapter that in the modern world where we have to maintain a lot of things at the same time it is very much possible for us to get frustrated and stressed out. And if you are a person that really worries about being perfect and maintaining all the stuff properly then it is really important that you keep your anger in a proper check. The adrenaline that is going to be flowing through your bloodstream, due to any angry situation, is going to make your anxiety and your psychological condition regarding it worse over time.

Doesn't matter if we are talking about anxiety or even psychological condition or any other physical condition or even depression. Anger has its bad effect upon all of these. Like I said, even if anger doesn't do any damage to you, then the guilty feeling that you are going to be facing after your angry state has passed by, is definitely going to leave you scarred.

Let me tell you a story from my personal life. There was once a time when I was facing a lot of problem regarding communicating with my family. You know, how often teenagers get into trouble with their parents

Anger management workbook for men

regarding their change of age and hormonal imbalances. Whenever I was getting mad at my parents due to something that I wanted and it was not happening, I was quite out bursting with anger several times a day. The major problem was that, my parents are really nice and they never think anything bad about me due to my yelling and being mad at them. The problem started, when after a couple of hours, my brain has entered a cool state, I started feeling guilty for all the things that I have said and all the things that I've done. That guilty feeling used to kill me from the inside. And that is exactly the worst part about getting angry.

It is more likely to happen that people have been facing trouble regarding managing their anger and other existing negative emotions inside their brain. The problem is that anger is more likely to be seen by many people and considered as one of the acceptable negative emotions to display. But that obviously does never mean that they are going to be responding well when someone else is displaying a lot of anger towards them.

And the reason that I have mentioned women in the title of this book is that they are the worst victims of this issue. Because of a genetically developed history, being the class of mother, women have a tendency to sacrifice their own expectations in order to achieve something that is big and great for the family. But that does never mean that women are not facing any type of negative emotion or anxiety or even anger. Problem is that, 90% of the time they suppress their anger inside themselves. They do this because they want to keep the family within a peaceful state and lost just lash out about every single mistake that has been made by someone. Of course, this has been done with a really noble point of view. Little did they know, this suppressed state of anger

Anger management workbook for men

creates a lot of other negative emotions inside a human brain that results severe and impulsive reactions in the future.

Maybe that is one of the reason that the rate of divorce is getting so high in this world.

In this book I will be address in directly towards all the problems related to anger management issues for both teenagers and also women. But like all the other books I will not be focusing my entire research and knowledge upon only these two facts. I will be discussing in an universal manner so that everyone can be benefited from the knowledge that I am sharing in this book.

Anger management workbook for men

CHAPTER 2: REASONS AND TRIGGERS FOR ANGER OUTBURSTS IN PEOPLE

In the chapter, we will be discussing a lot about the details about anger and how and why it is caused inside a person.

Let's get into the scientific explanation about the emotion named anger first.

If you go along with the dictionary meaning of anger than we can say that anger is basically a strong feeling of this pleasure and rejection aroused by something wrong.

The basic definition might not sound so bad as it might seem but it obviously does not give any detailed information about what exactly happens inside a person when he or she is under the situation of facing those same feelings of hostility and also getting a lot of strong emotions for rejection. Charles Spielberger, one of the world's most popular psychologist, who is basic field of research was the emotion named anger has been defining this term as a specific emotional state that varies from person to person in terms of intensity. These various levels of intensity might be from mild and simple irritation towards intense levels of furious state and rage.

With all the discussion that has been going throughout this book till now, might make you think that anger is really bad and also one should never have anger inside his mind. That is the exact problem where people start doing mistakes. Anger is completely normal to have and also none of the informative content or this book is

Anger management workbook for men

telling you that you shall never face anger and it is really bad if you are angry. What I am trying to teach and make you understand, is that despite of being one of the most normal emotions to have, you need to work on your perspective and also your mental exercises so that anger is not able to take over you and make you do things that you never wished to do.

You might have a question in your mind regarding the purpose of anger's existence. it is very hard and complicated properly understand the basic purpose of anger. If you have ever tried to work on a car engine or any other automobile engine then you know already that, it can be really one of the most overwhelming task and with a lot of components to handle you might easily get frustrated with it. Once you have mastered and properly understand the functions of each of the components that are available in front of you, the things will quickly starts to fall into their own place and you'll have a clear picture in front of you. Anger should be dealt with the exact same point of approach. When we our first trying are making our attempts to grasp the very meaning of the purpose of anger, the overall task might seem quite impossible to master.

But, as we are making slow and steady progress throughout all the steps and stages that are there to be understood, will slowly start to understand the fact that anger Management is actually far less overwhelming from which we have been thinking about it. Anger can be caused because of two different events occurring in front of you. One is internal events and the other is external events. Internal event is basically caused by the person himself. It can be as simple as thinking about some bad memories are thinking about something that really makes a person angry from the inside. The second type is

Anger management workbook for men

external events. Is quite as same as the first one but the only difference is that the cause of action has not been done by the individual himself rather than it has been done by someone else.

Understanding the cause of anger

Trying to manage our anger and also get into a peaceful state of mind it is very much important that we try to find the proper cause of our anger. This cannot be achieved without any practical experiments done on yourself. Imagine that you are getting angry at someone or something or someone that has been done wrongly in front of you, and you have already shown a lot of anger towards it. Is more like it happened that you are not going to be trying to think about it at a later time because you are going to be thinking that whenever you think about it will be a waste of your time and also it will ruin your good mood. This ignorance towards thinking about the angry station at a later time is exactly what does the most harm towards a human personality. Because it doesn't matter how much it is capable of ruining your mood but if you are not facing it with a logical explanation and also a open-minded perspective you are not going to be able to truly understand and also be able to get rid of it.

Imagine that you are angry at something and after a couple of hours when you have totally cooled down. Whenever that thought about your angry state comes into your mind you try your best to suppress that thought and not to think about it because you suspect and fear that is going to be ruining your good mood and it is going to be making you angry once again. But if you are avoiding the state of anger constantly and also not thinking about how everything started in the first place

Anger management workbook for men

then how do you expect that you are going to be able to find the root of your anger?

Whenever such type of thought comes inside your mind after any angry impulsive reaction, let it come. Don't just fight it. Try to face your thoughts. And when you do, it is possible that you might feel angry once again. But being angry is not the main focus point of this task. The main task is that whenever you thinking about the previous thing that you have given impossible reaction to, think about the exact situation and the exact scenario from which everything started in the first place. Think about the exact thing and the nature of that thing that made you mad at the first place. You will have a far better understanding about what and what type of thing is making you mad all the time. There is one thing done. Now for the second part, you need to properly understand the nature of the incident that has made you angry. Try to understand whether or not every single element or every single incident containing the same nature has been able to make you angry or not. If every single event with the same nature makes you angry, basically means that you hate that type of situation or that type of work being done in front of you. If the case is that, you are not feeling angry by the same type of incidents done by any other person, basically means that areas that single individual who did the wrong thing in front of you in the first place, whom you really despite of. It basically means that the same type of incident is actually not being able to make you angry rather than it is only the first person who did it. That means that the first person who made you angry was the only person that is hated by you. Not the incident or even not the nature of the incident.

When you are thinking about all of these, it is very much possible that imagining the entire scenario

Anger management workbook for men

happening in front of your eyes all over again might be able to make you angry from the inside. It's able to make you angry from the inside whenever you are totally alone sitting in your bedroom. Don't just try to fight it and get rid of the uncomfortable situations inside your mind. Once you face it with courage and a clear point of view, you will have a far better time about understanding and facing your fears.

It is more likely to be happening that your anger seems to just simply explode without any type of previous warning and exactly this makes it really difficult and complex to manage properly. Even if you have explosive anger which basically means that you will not be able to identify whether or not you are getting angry by any event. It is still possible that you might be able to prevent such type of explosion happening. all existing types of episodes related to anger explosion are basically following a common operator bill pattern. A proper examination about your own pattern is really the most and the first important step towards achieving a better management and a better control towards your anger related issues. It will really be quite useful for you to have a little look at your condition and also your reactions out of your angry state from this point of view. Every single person has develop their own personal patterns and methods of expressing anger and experiencing the feeling inside your brain. When you are able to understand the unique features of your personality related to your anger outcomes then it will be way too much easier for you to make the necessary changes that will be helpful for controlling your automatic reactions.

Anchor sequence inside any personality basically starts with a specific event that is known as the trigger of anger. A trigger can be everyday situations as simple as a

Anger management workbook for men

simple this agreement or even a speech of disrespect or even a struggle about what to do or how to achieve a certain thing. A lot of people become angry just about the type of relationship of the events happening around them. A trigger can be done either by yourself or even a trigger can be caused due to other people's negative behavior around you. Such type of negative behavior can be as simple as someone not being willing to hear what you have inside your head or even just being too much persuasive for what they want from you.

The second element that causes anger is the thoughts which are embedded with the triggered element. Whenever a specific set of event is able to make a person angry, which is basically known as a trigger, it is possible that there is going to be a certain point of view of seeing the entire event from the mind of the person who is getting angry.

When you have properly understood the reason and the trigger material for your anger it is now time for you to properly understand how you have been reacting whenever you are angry. If you don't have a clear idea about exactly how your face looks like whenever you're angry try making your angry face or try getting angry by saying the exact thing that you hate the most to yourself in front of a mirror. This will be able to give you a clear picture about how you exactly look and how you exactly feel in front of the other person whenever you are angry. This will be able to create a sense of fear inside your mind about your own self that if you get angry you are such type of a bad person and your mind will automatically start to reject such type of event from happening in the first place.

There will be a lot more detailed discussion about how to make your own profile to analyze your

Anger management workbook for men

personality and come up with the best approach to get rid of anger Management related issues.

Let's just take into a little bit more theoretical part. I know that theoretical part is always going to read rather than just knowing about the solution itself in the first hand. But the problem is that, you need to learn properly in order to understand and come up with a solution that is going to be best for your own unique situation.

After this next chapter of some theoretical discussion we will be diving straight into the practical aspects about how and why and in which way you should be managing your anger.

Anger management workbook for men

CHAPTER 3: MANAGING YOUR EMOTIONS

To be honest, I do realise that the title of this chapter is getting more on the dramatic side rather than on the factual side. But that is all for good reason. You might be wondering by this part of this book that we are almost down to 1/3 of this book already and we have not yet discussed any of the actual "solutions" to the problem that actually started the topic of this book. Which is basically how to get a proper grip on the control of your anger while being a parent and also while maintaining all of the duties of parenthood. But trust me when I say this, whenever any problem arises, you are going to see a lot of content, a lot of different suggestions about how to solve the problem period but very less discussion and emphasis is actually given on the actual source and how the problem actually generates from really small things and takes form into something much bigger. If we together start to understand and realise and put proper emphasis on the points which actually causes the problem, then solving the problem would have been much easier and also it would take much less effort than it was taking in the prior times period

That is why, up until this chapter and the next chapter, we will be discussing mainly on the sources and how the problem generates and spreads throughout different aspects of our life of being a parent. And in this chapter, will be discussing three major points for parenthood anger management. That is the sources of the anger also known as the triggers that are usual and also common for most of the parents around the world. And as

Anger management workbook for men

we are speaking about different triggers, we made sure that we cover the entire topic in a rather universal manner. You might be thinking that why do we need to cover this in a specifically universal manner? The reason is pretty simple. The thing is that, different cultures and different parts of the world have different types of problems and social aspects. As in Western countries such as the United kingdom's, United States, Canada, Mexico, Europe and similar other countries, living with your parents after the age of 15 or 16 is considered as quite a disgrace. And another thing is that living with your parents is not a common culture in the aforesaid countries. On the other hand, throughout the eastern parts of the world, The situation is quite different.

Because on the eastern sides, countries such as Japan, China, Indonesia, Malaysia, India, Bangladesh and similar other countries, the culture of living with your parents even after you are quite adult enough is actually going on from beyond time and history. And as much as us, people from the western part of the world, would say that this is quite abnormal and unnatural. The same goes for the other way around period to them, our way of letting our child go at such young age and also not living with your parents and your entire family as a one single group is quite different as well. That is why, at the beginning of this book, I told you about not comparing yourselves with one another rather than just focusing on the main thing that you have to do.

As this chapter is mainly designed up on three main topics which are firstly, triggers that are usual and common. Secondly, cause of stress for trigger to take effect. Thirdly, some personal stories to explain even more which you need to understand on this topic.

Anger management workbook for men

Triggers that are usual and common

To be honest, you will get a feeling that the subject matter of this part of this chapter has been already discussed in a previous chapter. But when you actually finish reading this chapter, you will realize that they are not the same at all and they are quite the opposite from one another period

In this part, we will be discussing about the common triggers that actually caused the stress factor to explode and also you to lash out in such a way that is never acceptable either on a social or on a personal basis.

Whenever a person is being a parent for the first time or even for the second or third or fourth time, it is never the same or it is never predictable. Each experience is unique from one another and also each of the person or persons that I am talking about faces unique experience from one another as well.

And that is the most complicated and maybe one of the most serious parts about human life and specially about parenthood. And that is, there is absolutely no guideline or no rulebook that you can follow in order to get a better hand and also on a better grip of the entire situation. And as much as this is a problem, I personally think that it is a blessing from the nature as well. As I always like to discuss any topic for any of my books on a skeptical and rather universal manner so that everyone from every sort of belief can relate themselves. Same goes for this book as well.

First, let me discuss it on a rather spiritual and religious level. If you are a person that believes in the

Anger management workbook for men

creator or in other words that you believe in a specific God that has created this world and also created us, you would of course understand this part without any hesitation. That is, God has created this world end the entire nature in such a way in also in such harmony that everything balances itself out at the end of the day. The only thing that creates the imbalance and the only thing that actually creates the confusion and delusional situation is the part of mankind itself. Apart from the Science fiction stories and all of the Super villain movies that you might see on your local Starbucks, it is quite true that it doesn't matter how well structured and how well planned you are with your life, at the end of the day, if you take the human form out of the entire structure of nature, nature would have been at its best peak situation. Now, emphasizing to the part of where I said that everything has its own purpose and everything balances out itself, we need to put proper focus on our duties rather than focusing on other people so that we are capable of staying at the best performance of our necessity.

Some of the triggers that are really going to be common for almost any type of person and also from any type of custom or religious background are going to be discussed down below. To start with, the first thing that actually ignites the fire of anger and also makes a person burst out from the stress and from all of the anger that has been built up slowly overtime is going to be definitely not something that you would have think of.

It is actually the small criticism that you might receive from another person on a totally irrelevant matter. You might be thinking and also be quite confused about the "irrelevant" word. Let me explain it to you. The thing is that, whenever you are talking with another person about totally a different topic rather than being a parent. In such

Anger management workbook for men

a situation, let me give you a small example and also and imaginary scenario so that you can understand the situation even better.

Imagine that you are a person that really admires bikes or muscle cars or anything in general that has your special point of interest. For the sake of this conversation, let's just assume that you are a person that is really into Harley-Davidson custom bikes. Now, you are also a person that has proper expertise on building custom bikes for yourself and also you are a well known person for modification done over the side bikes.

Now, imagine that you have prepared a total custom project for yourself, consider that as a dream project of yours period now whenever you are talking to another person or even to a friend about the project after or while it is being completed period of course, this topic or this subject matter of the conversation that you are just having has nothing to do with being a parent or also anything to do with the factors of parenthood neither it is remotely related any possible way in this world with parenthood.

That part, is totally understandable. But on the other hand, as you are a parent at the same time, you might be getting a lot of stress at home and also at work at the same time while you are constantly suppressing it sometimes consciously sometimes unconsciously.

Whenever you are really tired and you just got home from work, and suddenly your newborn baby starts crying, you are never angry at the baby. And even if you are, it basically means that you are a really bad person. So as assuming that you are not a really demonic person and you are totally sympathetic to your child and to the situation and you are accepting the fact that the child

Anger management workbook for men

crying at such late hour has nothing to do anything for any people on an intentional basis.

But, at the same time it is also the true fact that you are obviously quite stressed as you just got home from work period that is why, some small things that are not actually capable of making us angry, creates a certain amount of stress inside us. For certain reasons, which we keep suppressed inside ourselves period now, this goes on and on for days after days. And at a certain time, you might be starting to feeling a little light headed and sometimes a little down all the time. At the same time, on a totally irrelevant and totally unnecessary object, you might lash out with all your mind and all your force and all of the stress that you have been building up until this time.

Now, back to what I was saying. As you are talking to a friend about the newly made by that you have just finished with all that hard work and all those late night shifts. Imagine that there is actually a flaw in the design that might cause some problems in the comfort or the experience of riding the bike or even there is just simply a minor flaw about the looks of it. And as your friend just says something negative not in the offensive way but rather to actually make you focus on the things so that you can make it even better than before. But even in that situation, all of the stress that had been slowly building up inside you day after day, will burst out, that even if it doesn't; It has a chance of bursting out on similar small events that has nothing to do with the actual stress itself.

And that is when, the most tricky and most complicated part of this entire chapter comes in. And that is to either go In TWO direction.

Anger management workbook for men

The first one, is in question, is about mainly autosuggestion ING and training yourself in such a way that you are automatically able to control your psychological factors in such a way that you have absolutely no problem of controlling such type of sudden outbursts.

One of the most important things about human psychology and maintaining human psychology that we usually take for granted and also ignore a lot is to talk to ourselves about the problem that we have and also think within ourselves inside our mind about the problems that needs to be solved. We think usually that such type of problems are so small that it doesn't actually needs any attention and putting attention towards it is basically a waste of our time. But as it seems, judging by the current situation of the world and also the current statistics that have been surveyed from different countries and also data from different type of people who have been suffering from stress and anxiety proves the total opposite. It seems that the small things that we usually take for granted and also we think that it is such small that putting attention to it will be a total waste of time. Has actually the capability of destroying our entire mentality and also our psychological balance that we usually strive for.

If you continuously autosuggestion your brain and also tell yourself that certain type of things are bound to make you triggered to lash out of anger and you need to control yourself. You have a comparatively higher chance of being able to stay in control while you are constantly facing such situations with actually the possibility of bursting out in anger.

The second one, before actually telling this I need to tell you something more about the first one first.

Anger management workbook for men

The thing is that, the first one, might be the most helpful but it has comparatively less chance of being efficient and also giving you the proper results that you want.

Now, let's jump to the second one. The second one actually demands that you be open to the people that you usually communicate with the situations that you are facing. In such type of scenario even if you are facing any unfortunate event in which you are lashing out or bursting out of anger and you are unable to hold yourself or control yourself up until a social aspect. You will still have the sympathy and also the understanding of the people that you are going through a tough time and also you are quite stressed out from the inside and the recent outburst of anger that the other person has just experienced has nothing to do on a personal level and it was totally not targeted and caused because of their actions.

There are some people who might argue with me about this sympathetic part. And you might tell me that being such attention seeker and sympathy seeker is not actually good for a personality. Now, it might be totally true or it might be totally false. Whether it is true or false is not actually relevant in this case. The main relevant point or the main relevancy that I'm actually trying to tell you about is that which works for you best and which gives you the most efficient output for the effort that you are giving to yourself to make yourself better. Even if it makes you a little bit of sympathy seeker and even if you are actually telling your weaknesses to other people, if it actually helps and gets the job done, then I absolutely see no harm at all. To be honest, I am a person, that is willing to lose a little bit of my ego if it actually helps me. There is an old Chinese saying that to give something, you must lose something. And that is exactly how the entire world

Anger management workbook for men

works. And that is also how the theory of the balance of nature actually works. If you are not giving anything, you cannot expect anything in return. You might think that there are actually people and even you have faced some situations in which you are only getting and not giving at all full stuff but to be honest, at certain stage of life, you will realize that you have been wrong for the most part of your life and despite the fact that you did not give to get something in return at some stage, it will have a long lasting effect at some other stage of your life at the same time.

So, being open to the people that you are mostly closed with and also being open to the same people about the stress and the type of situation that you are facing about controlling your anger helps you a lot in terms of maintaining the situation and also reducing the stress after you have lashed out with anger in a certain situation. Let me explain to you with some more stories in this case. Imagine that you have just lashed out to a person due to some small negative things that they might have said. Now what they have said might have been negative and also might deserve a little negative reaction but the way that you reacted was totally overreacting and totally overdoing it all over again. If you have been actually open to that person that type of stress and the type of situation that you are currently going through, and if you have been open to that person about your certain and sudden outbursts of anger, then you can easily apologize to that person right after you have just lashed out with anger and also explained that it was not personal and you are totally sorry for what happened and they would totally understand. But if you did not explain to them prior to that point, any explanations made later to the event would only harm the relationship and do absolutely no good at all.

Anger management workbook for men

And also at the same time, As you have already expressed about how you are feeling right now about all of the stress and all of them being a new parent for the first time or even for whichever time it is, you are going to be having a comparatively comfortable time with explaining why you have actually lashed out. And at the same time, on the other person, he or she will be able to understand you much better than what it was before.

Emotion

Emotion, in its most broader sense of explanation is nothing but a chemical reaction inside our brain which creates a sensation of different type of feelings on a physical and mental state.

Anger is also just like all the other emotions. It creates a specific chain of reaction regarding the release of some specific hormone from our brain into our blood flow which makes us feel in a specific way. Just like all the other emotions anger works in the same pattern of just getting throughout the entire bloodstream with its hormone and making our physical and psychological reaction in a specific way.

Let's just simply begin with the very basic definition of water motions truly are. Emotions are basically a physical and mental state of our existence generated by our brain and some specific hormone that is capable of motivating us to take a proper type of action and also energize the embedded behavior along with it. emotions may be conscious or even subconscious and sometimes totally unconscious inside our brain. Which basically means that, you can have a strong existence of emotion inside your brain without you even knowing it.

Anger management workbook for men

Emotions have the capability to slowly lingering in the background of our minds just like and orchestra playing a soft ambient music in the distance. On the other hand emotions also have the capability to feel like a heavy metal concert blasting write in your ears and insisting you to provide proper attention and also listen to them. Emotion has a various range of it's effectivity.

The difference between having a specific mood and a specific emotion is that emotion as a temporary and short-term blast of feelings inside our psychological state were as if that psychological state stage for a longer time is called a specific mood.

To be honest, both of them are the exact same thing. Just their nature and their time span of sticking on to you defines what they are.

Emotions are basically divided into two basic types. Depending upon the age which they are first emerging inside the human brain. The first one is basically the primary emotions such as anger, fear, joy, sadness, surprise and disgust. Primary emotions are more likely to be one of the essential elements for a human personality in order to survive properly with a balance life. All of these emotions have different type of reaction on the outer side of a human personality. We can say that anger has a common reaction to fight or to move against the opposition or sometimes even to violently attacked the party in front of the person. Whereas on the other hand fear has a completely different type of reaction on the outer side of a human personality with basically consists of the intention of the tendency to escape of leaf from the scene. Just like these two that I have told you, all the emotions that I have discussed in the primary section have different type of reactions. To be honest this is one of the most basic things that you don't even need to learn. You

Anger management workbook for men

already know that if you are angry you are willing to step forward and find the person and if you are scared that you are willing to just run away. You don't need a book or any other informative content to teach to you. let's get into some more in detailed discussion which is less likely for you to know on a normal life.

The second category of emotion is the social emotions which basically consists of shame, guilt, embarrassment, pride, etc.

The reason for us having emotions

The explanation is completely scientific and biological. And if you want a simple word of explanation that I can tell you that the entire reason for having such type of emotion is only for the sake of our survival. If I'm putting in faces on the biological and the scientific explanation about the reason of why do we have emotions, I can tell you that it's all about the hormones and the chemical inside our brain and our blood stream. Different type of situation and different type of sensation forces our brain to release different types of hormone and chemicals into our bloodstream which makes us react.

Just like whenever you are excited with a lot of happiness it is more likely that you will be shaking your head and hand in a really fast pace, similarly whenever you are angry, it is more likely that your muscles and your jaw line is going to be so tensed up that sometimes it's going to be hurting after you are not angry anymore. Every single emotion inside our biological condition controls a specific set of reactions on a psychological and on a physical basis.

Anger management workbook for men

How is our own emotion distracting us from what needs to be done?

just after reading the title of this paragraph you might already have a little vision from a scientific movie. Science fiction movies to be exact. Sometimes we watch step of movies on the television or even in the theatres that in a distant future Time When everything is so technological and so scientific people are telling each other that having emotion is nothing but a waste of time and so on.

No, that is exactly the opposite of what I am trying to tell you. Without emotions humans are not humans. It is only the existence of emotions and emotional pattern of thinking that makes us best among all the living creatures in this world. Because the capability of judgement along with our emotion is the only thing that makes a superior and also far better than any other living species in order to survive and to adapt. But it is not necessarily true that all of the emotions that we have inside our biological existence is important or useful for us. But as like all the famous philosophers have said, if there was not the existence of darkness, people would never have valued the existence of light. Just like that, if you really want to appreciate all the good emotions and all the good things in humanity you need to learn and also exist with the bad sides of it too.

But the problem is that it is more likely to happen in a lot of people that they fail to properly understand the necessity to get rid of the negative emotions as soon as possible. And for those who are actually aware of the necessity to get rid of the negative emotions make the mistakes of understanding as changing

Anger management workbook for men

the perspective with just suppressing the negative emotions inside themselves. I know that the last two sentences have been way too much complicated. Allow me to explain.

There are two types of people who are in the majority of the entire population around the world. Either people are not being able to understand that they need to put proper attention towards the negative emotion and proper steps needs to be taken to get rid of them. Or, in the other hand, people are thinking about it in just the wrong way. Just like any other chemical reaction existing in this physical world every single element of emotion inside as a linked with one another that controls our overall wellbeing and balance of life.

Imagine that you do not have any problems related to anxiety or depression or sadness. But somehow, you are getting really angry repeatedly at some action or some incidents done by someone in front of you. There's going to be a certain time when you just lash out with your full anger at that person. After couple of hours when you have actually calmed yourself down, you will be now facing a series of rough emotions inside you. Despite of not having any type of problems related to anxiety or depression you will now be facing a lot of guilt feelings inside your mind that you have behaved really harshly with the person earlier. That one little thought "things could have been done in a different" will slowly start to kill you from the inside. It will reduce your happiness, it will reduce your joy, it will reduce your effectiveness and efficiency for the works that you need to do on a regular basis. I hope that you are being able to see that one single negative emotion has been capable of triggering a whole series of other emotions.

Anger management workbook for men

And this is exactly how one negative emotion has been capable of triggering a total series of reaction inside our brain and reducing our overall balance of life.

Why understanding emotion is important?

As we have been talking a lot about what emotions really are, and how each different emotional has its own set of reactions, it is now time for us to understand why all this study is really important for us.

As I've been telling you from the very beginning of this book that if you really want to get rid of a problem you need to get to the root of it and to understand it properly you need a complete study about how and what the entire problem is all about. If you really want to understand what type of emotion your feelings from inside and you are quite a bit confused about it you need to know that there is not a single book or any other informative content nor any other counselor or professional psychologist can help you with this. The only thing that can truly help you from the inside is your own conscience and how you have been able to understand yourself and your pattern of behavior on the exterior level. I do understand that it is not just as easy as I am saying this in this book. But if it was really that easy you wouldn't have needed the help of any other person rather than yourself to solve it, right?

You need to give yourself proper amount of time and also think about all the things that you have done and try your best to understand how you are actually feeling when you were in the action of doing all those events. Imagine that you have just had a fight with your friend at school and now in the evening when you are sitting in

Anger management workbook for men

your bedroom you are thinking about that incident on exactly how everything happened. The next thing that I am about to tell you might solve almost all of your problems. If you don't want any further discussion you might get a feeling that you don't need to read any more for the into this book because you have already got an the biggest answer to all the questions. But if you really need a sustainable solution for the problem that you have, then you need to complete the whole study on this book.

As I was saying, in the evening you are sitting at your bedroom thinking about all the events that happened today at school. when you remember each of the second of that event and you are going through the entire scenario just like your watching a movie, you will be easily able to spot out some certain events or some certain stage where you made a decision inside your head to react. When you are sitting in your room and thinking about all the scenarios one after another, you will be easily able to spot the decisions and how you would have done it totally in a different way. At that point, when you . that you should have taken that decision instead of this one, those words that you are thinking in your head will stay inside your head and it will obviously help you to guide in a similar situation in the future and act in the most rational way possible.

Anger management workbook for men

CHAPTER 4: BASIC LESSONS OF ANGER MANAGEMENT

Starting with the basics of anger Management

What type of person or what type of personality that you have, will not be defining what type of person that you are. The main element that is going to be defining you as a person or even as a human being is how well you have been able to behave under pressure. There are a lot of certain situations in which we feel way too much frustrated body when stressed out in such a way that we are not able to control our basic emotion and also we lash out with impulsive reactions in terms of some certain imbalance happening in front of us. I am not telling you that if you lash out with anger and such type of other impossible reaction in a situation where you have been mistreated in such a way that is beyond imagination, it is not good at all. Rather than trying to tell you that instead of lashing out with anger if you try to manage yourself in such a way that you are able to look at this situation that is making you mad in a different perspective it will be able to help you calm down easily. Having anger or getting angry at something does not mean that you are a bad person or you have any type of negative characteristics in your personality. And that is exactly why I am not telling you that you should never get angry. The main thing that I have been trying to tell you and that I want you and need you to understand that getting angry is not something that should not be done ever, rather than you should focus on how you can control your reaction and look at the

Anger management workbook for men

situation from a different perspective so that you are able to keep an open mind and try to get a better understanding about what is happening.

When you are starting your practical lessons or even your practical working exercise to manage your anger on a perfect base is you need to make your own profile so that you understand your own characteristics at the first place. Just like I have told you in the previous part of this book, the same method will not be working on two different person. Because every single person has their own unique and different way of thinking and different way of reacting towards different situations. And that is exactly why, doesn't matter how many counselors or how many psychological therapy that you have gone through, you need to understand yourself by yourself first before actually getting help from some other source. And that is why the most important part about anger Management is getting a profile of yourself about how you react to different circumstances and what triggers you the most.

Making your own profile

This is the first step that you need to do if you really want to create a proper management of your anger and of course in the most efficient way. whenever you are trying to create your own profile you need to keep an open mind towards the information that you receive by studying on yourself. The first thing that you would want to do is to try to picture yourself as an angry person and try to imagine every single scene of the situation whenever you are angry and reacting to someone else. identify the small little details in your personality whenever you are lashing out with anger. Just like a movie scene, imagine yourself acting out all the things that you

Anger management workbook for men

do whenever you are angry. When you have done that, try to identify every single action that you are doing and come up with any alternative approach or any alternative reaction that you could have given. This will give you a draught idea about what type of reaction can you use to replace the impossible reaction whenever you are angry. I know that whenever you are angry this might be quite impossible to remember about how you should react to something that you really despise of. But the truth is, after a certain amount of time, you will be able to automatically think about the alternatives reactions apart from just lashing out and dealing with your anger outbursts. This will help you to keep a proper guideline in front of your eyes which you can use to identify what type of behavior or what type of reaction should be used instead of just yelling out what you are feeling inside.

After the point when you have identified the alternative approach towards a certain incident that has been making you angry, you need to give yourself a lot of time to think about those situations which you can avoid and handle in a specific way. Let me tell you a practical story and example for a better understanding about this point.

Imagine yourself in a situation where one of your friends has done something that really makes you angry. So angry that you just want to kill that person with your words. Now just inside your head, start thinking about every single details of the scenario and how you would have acted out in such type of situation. At this point, start thinking about the alternative methods and the alternative type of approach or even perspective towards the whole situation. You will be able to find out a lot of different perspectives about the same situation and at this point you will be also having the feeling that the entire thing

Anger management workbook for men

that you have been so mad about is totally useless. I do recognize that there are a certain amount of situation where there are absolutely nothing that you can do to avoid the anger. Apart from the inevitable, you can use this method to think about different situations that usually make you angry in the practical life. For example, let's say that there are only two things in this world that makes you angry. The first one is leaving your shoes off at a place that it is not appropriate, and the second one is not finishing the bottle of juice. I know this sounds way too much childish but let's just imagine this for the sake of discussion and explanation. Imagine that these are the only two things that have been able to make you really angry and lash out with impulsive reaction towards someone else. Now, what you really need to do is, think about such type of scenario where you have been facing the exact same circumstances. Just imagine the entire scene happening right in front of your eyes as a movie scene. Thinking about the entire scenario over and over again will give you different perspective about the circumstances it also you will be able to think about it from a different point of view. This will help you in terms of creating a proper profile of your anger management situation inside your mind. From that, you will be easily able to identify what are the exact small details that make you angry and what type of situation leaves the biggest impact inside your mind.

Managing your life style

When we are trying to look for the reasons of our anger there is a large possibility that most of us are not going to be giving proper consideration towards our lifestyle and also how the environmental factors are existing around us. In this part of this chapter I will be

Anger management workbook for men

trying to make you look at your habits and environmental elements as the first step towards reducing your reactions with anger.

Let's talk about your habits and some factors related to the environment around you. I know that this might sound a little bit funny, but have you ever given proper thoughts towards the effect of whether that you have on your personality and also sometimes how you are able to interact with other people around you?

Despite of the fact that this sounds really not so important, but it is indeed one of the most important factors that control your mood and your intention towards taking different types of reaction. Several research information from the University of Columbia have already shown us that a certain temperature of the weather has the capability to create a large number of agreeability and also emotional stability and avoiding any type of introversion. If you take proper consideration about the environmental and the weather facts and its effect on your personality then you will be easily able to identify the negative impacts that the rough weather has on you and you will also be able to stay aware about the fact that such weather has been laying down a certain amount of negative impact on your personality and you will be able to easily identify and avoid any type of impulsive reactions arising out of this reason.

Your food habit and your overall nutrition status inside your body may also have a large amount of impact for how you have been able to react towards different situation. Physiologists have already shown as proven data that imbalanced nutrition and also high intake of carbohydrate has been capable of creating imbalance of hormonal existence inside your body resulting as

Anger management workbook for men

impulsive reactions and sometimes instability towards other people's opinion.

There are a lot of people, even myself, who faces a lot of problem if we are hungry. Hungry doesn't mean just starving and craving for food. Hunger can even be caused due to some small amount of grazing for a certain snack or even a drink that you really love. If you have the tendency to eat a certain food at a certain time, be sure that you do not miss that food because that will be able to create an imbalance state inside your mind and also make you not capable of giving proper reactions.

Sleep has the largest amount of impact of our personality regarding how well we have been able to keep our mood in a good state. To be honest, you need to provide proper attention towards how much sleep you are getting and also how much of that time of sleep is considered as a healthy sleep. Sleep problems are more likely to be one of the important reasons in terms of violence from any intimate partner or even getting bullied at school sometime cyber bullying and social harassment. the worst part about is that we are not able to identify the exact reason of any type of sleeping disorders. What we can actually do is to predict a higher possibility reason that has the most chances of being true in your case for which you might not have been able to get a sufficient amount of sleep. But one of the major parts about getting a healthy amount of sleep is to maintain your proper lifestyle and physical activity along with a proper balanced diet for yourself. Actually, if you are able to get a proper routine for your food chart then already you will be able to get much better sleep at a regular basis. Work is one of the important factors that influence our habits of sleeping. Back in 2014, a server down upon the major parts of the United States of America has shown that more than 21

Anger management workbook for men

persons of adult people who have been surveyed inside United States have reported that they work more than 50-59 hours per week. It is true that many adults at their working state have been working throughout the entire evening or even night or even with rotating shifts in the workplace but that is of course not good for a proper cycle of well maintained life. Due to the fact that financial needs actually will not be going up with how you want to sleep. But the truth is that doesn't matter what type of environment or what type of working profession that you are in, you need to give the highest priority towards a specific period of time throughout the entire day in which you can have a constant and sound sleep. Despite the fact that if your working schedule totally depends on how you are working at night it will not be able to give you as much efficiency that it should have. But if you can manage a certain amount of time in your regular routine that you will take a sound sleep doesn't matter if it is in the daytime or in the night time, it will be able to increase the condition of your mood towards the better way.

Creating a proper and well balanced lifestyle doesn't mean that you need to be spending a lot of time on yourself just making everything perfect. It basically means to keep an eye open for the smallest detail to cover up simply and make your life just one step better than it was before. Imagine that whenever you are getting home from your work at evening or even late at night, it will be really frustrating for you if you have to make your bed all over again ready just to get into it to your good night sleep. But if you take just a couple of minutes in the morning before rushing to work, so that you can clean up your bed after you have gotten up, this will create a huge sense of relief inside you whenever you are getting home from work that you do not need to make your bed again. The feeling that all you need to do is to just open your door get inside your

Anger management workbook for men

bedroom and throw yourself on your bed is may be the largest relief that a working person can have.

All you need to do is to look out for the small details so that you can create a well balance lifestyle and also you need to be attentive towards the small downsides of your lifestyle that you need to change. This will help you create a well detailed profile for yourself which can be used for later purposes of getting your anger management into a proper structure.

Anger management workbook for men

CHAPTER 5: PRACTICAL ASPECTS OF ANGER MANAGEMENT

I know that the previous chapter has already told you a lot of things about how to manage your anger and how to start on with danger management program. But you need more practical aspects and hands-on expertise in order to truly understand the entire process. In this chapter I will be delivering you exactly those information which you need the most. I do realize that doesn't matter whatever I am telling you the end product has to be done by you. You need to remember that doesn't matter what type of information or what type of book or exercise that you are following to manage your anger, the end will entirely depend upon how much you are able to commit yourself to the process and also willing to make yourself a better person than you are.

Just take a little bit time to understand this chapter properly and I promise you that you will be profited by a large margin for leading your life towards the goal that you always wish to accomplish. We had all quite well hour of the feeling that dealing with our inner anger is quite a hard task for us and also it is really difficult to properly manage it inside the boundaries. I also do recognize the fact that there are some situation in which anger can give you great results in terms of the efforts that you are putting in and also it will help you to keep up with your expectations. In any type of cases it is proven that anger that has the capability of damaging other people should obviously be overseen properly. There are a large number of strategies regarding anger management conducted over the patients by the doctors

Anger management workbook for men

or even psychological experts. If you are dealing with your anger then obviously it will help you to obtain the general public status of your personality. But there is a slight chance that whenever you are out bursting with anger it will leave a scar inside the other person's mind and also it will leave your personality and reputation jeopardized.

If you are an angry person then obviously your anger is going to be hurting you in terms of your overall well being on a psychological and also physical existence. You need to change the nature of your temper and also how fast you are willing to react to something by watching some mind soothing and decent film or even decent music and so on. I know that every person has his or her own taste in terms of media selection. You might be a serious metal head that listens to death metal and in fact it might be really possible that listening to heaven metal music or hard rock music makes you calm down and also relaxed. But that is only on the conscious level of your mind. If you didn't know this yet, we are only able to use 6% or 7% of our total brain as a conscious mind of our biological existence. the rest of the 93 or 94% of our brain usually works as our subconscious and our unconscious mind which operates our inner organs and sum of our inner senses which we also know as sixth sense. who's basically means that the type of heavy metal music or hard rock song that you have been listening for quite a long time might be able to relax yourself down on the conscious mind. But what about the rest of the 93% of your subconscious and unconscious mind? I'm not telling you to avoid any type of aggressive or hard metal type music. I'm not also telling you that such type of music is bad for you and you should not ever listen to them. What I'm basically trying to tell you is that on occasional basis you should listen to relaxing music such as acoustic or classical music that will be helpful for you to calm yourself down

Anger management workbook for men

on an interior level. Not only this, But also the relaxing music will be helpful for your inner brain to operate properly and also to think straight. For those who are really habituated to listening to hard music, I know that type of relaxing music will be way too much boring for you. But what would you prefer for yourself? Only think about what you are actually comfortable with or just sacrifice a little percentage of your time to invest into something that you don't like but it will obviously give you a lot of benefits?

I know that by logical explanation, The second one will be the most probable and the most rational answer to give. Despite of being so much obvious and so much lame, if something really has the capability of giving yourself the thing that you want then I don't understand what is the harm in doing that? Most people are so much willing to just focus on to what they love to do that they usually understand that they really need. And that is exactly the mistake that people are making all the time.

Relaxing music and soft story-based movies have the capability of relaxing your mind from the inside and also you will be able to reduce a lot of stress factors inside your daily behavior.

is that stuff of your event that you have been watching relaxing movies and listen to relaxing music you will be able to discuss with your companion or anyone off your family or your friends about your life, in such a way that, you will be able to understand and also explain a lot of things in much easier way rather than you had been doing in the past. Dismissal is one of the biggest trigger of any person in terms of getting his anger quite boosted up onto a certain level. This was so kind easy to disturb a man and also make them quite few years in terms of reaction and also decision making. If you really want to

Anger management workbook for men

manage our angers efficiently then we need to perceive the trigger and also figure out about how exactly we can adapt to such type of situation and such type of circumstances towards a better feeling and not just having anger inside us in terms of getting a reaction. The main mistake that more than 90% of people all around the world who have been suffering with anger management related issues make is that, whatever the circumstances or whatever the situation or whatever the event makes us angry we try our best to not think about them. Just like we have been hearing in movies and drama series, If you run away from your fears you are never going to be able to get better of it. If you really want to avoid and be capable of not being disturbed by something that has been disturbing you for quite a lot of time then you need to learn how to face it and you need to be facing it regularly by yourself so that you get habituated to it and also your reactions towards it becomes numb. Despite of the fact that my last sentence sounds really dumb, but this actually works. Just like whenever you are imagining a movies in inside your head, is you start to imagine and live in your imagination about those exact same events that have been capable of making you really angry than you will be slowly start to develop a feeling that such type of event is not quite important to you that you are going to reacting so seriously about it.

If you have gone to any type of counseling session or any psychologist for the betterment of your anger management related issues, You might have already noticed that all the psychologist or psychiatrist or any other mental doctor would ask you a lot of questions regarding the exact thing that has been making you really angry and the entire session towards you is going to be feeling really frustrating. it is true that people are often triggered with their highest amount of anger inside the

Anger management workbook for men

anger management program related sessions. But that is entirely done with purpose. Because whenever you are facing the exact same thing over and over again, you will be developing a sense of numbness inside your brain that you will not be willing to react towards it with the same excitement that you have been reacting to it earlier.

If you just take 30 minutes of time from every day of your life and think about the exact same events that has been making you really mad on someone or something, You will be easily able to develop yourself quite a lot by within just a couple of months. And by the term a couple of months I do not mean more than two months. I know this might sound really obvious and really simple and quite hard to believe that such type of easy approach towards anger can actually be helpful in terms of making you less angry.

But that is indeed the truth. Anger is basically a problem supposed towards a specific event that triggers your excitement in a certain way. If you are able to get used to those certain circumstances that has been capable of making you excited in this specific way then easily you will be able to manage your anger quite efficiently.

Whenever you are thinking all about the situation that has been incapable of making you angry You need to think the entire situation as this. What would happen if you do not just think about it? What would happen if you don't just care about it? What would happen if you don't give a single dime a value towards the event that has been making you angry? If you feel that you're being angry has been capable of doing some change of the entire situation, then still you have even the slightest reason of getting angry. But think about this, What if the entire situation can also have the same amount of outcome if you come yourself down and speak with a

Anger management workbook for men

soothing tone? What if just not reacting towards it makes everything stay still the same? If you learn to give yourself proper amount of value and also if you learn to value your own mood then you will be quite able to learn how to avoid some certain situations.

Let me tell you a story from my life. The story that I'm about to tell you is from a long time ago even before when I actually started my research or anger management. I was just a college student back then about to graduate in a couple of months. And to the entire time for me was quite frustrating with all the speech and presentation and all the other practical works that I had to submit within a programed amount of time. The problem was, I was not quite well habituated with the fact that I have to work with teammates in order to complete a task. But my course and my education was in such a way that I had to work in a group of 10 in order to submit my last project that was required to give me the passing mark of my graduation. I don't know why or I don't know how but every single member of my team was way too much lazy and also loves me and disrespectful towards the work that they have in their hand. I know some people might refer to me as a nerd guy. But I didn't get way too much. Because if being nerdy gives me just the thing that I want then I don't understand where's the harm in that. So as I was saying, back in that time I had to submit a specific project that required a lot of paperwork. And I was quite shocked that we all decided that a specific amount of time will be divided among all of the team members to complete the paperwork in a certain amount of time. But all of them were quite reckless and just not getting about the time limit. Every time I ask them about when they are going to be submitting the paperwork that they have been assigned to do, They would just simply say that chill out it will only take a couple of hours we will do it tomorrow. This was

Anger management workbook for men

really pissing me off. The reason was that I was quite a perfectionist back then. I mean I'm still just like that right now. But back then I was quite young and also quite naive towards the amount of patients that I need to have inside my personality. I was constantly failing to understand that the amount of dedication or the amount of hardworking tendency that I have inside my mind is really important to have inside everyone's personality. But the truth is that only a handful amount of people among the entire population truly possess that characteristic. I was also failing to understand that if I have dedication on a specific matter that doesn't signify the fact that the other person in front of me is going to feel the same amount of dedication towards the same thing. And just because of this, and the type of quiet person that I was, I was not being able to react to them or even force them to complete the task in the certain time. But I was getting quite furious and angry from the inside. I was yelling inside myself all the time that why on God's earth can someone be so much reckless and careless about the responsibilities. Not just why but especially how. This was really messing my whole head from the inside. I was facing so much frustration at that time that even the easiest course that I had in my list, I did not even get the proper score that I usually used to have. I started to realize after that time, Even if my group members are not performing properly this will not hamper my score and even my yelling and getting frustrated about the entire thing that they are not doing the work properly has not giving me any benefit or even it is not doing me any harm. At that time, I asked myself that, why am I stressing myself so much about this then? Because the thing is, every member of the group will have their individual scoring in terms of the final result and also if any group member of our team does something wrong that will not hamper the score of the other members. So why should I care and bother myself so much regarding

Anger management workbook for men

what they have not been able to do? I could have just simply ignore the entire fact and this would have saved me a lot of time. Not only the time, But also the amount of stress and frustration and the good mood that I usually used to have whenever I was working on a project. It's actually at that moment, I started to realize that I need to understand the true value of something and to determine and come up with a result that whether or not getting stressed out about that thing is worth it.

I hope that you understanding exactly what I'm trying to tell you.

The whole purpose behind telling you the story was only to make you understand about the perspective which you have been taking in terms of looking towards a specific circumstance. You need to give proper thought about the exact event that makes you really angry. Because whenever you are living that exact moment of your anger inside your mind over and over again you will be able to see a lot of hidden perspectives and a lot of hidden things that you haven't been able to see at the moment of your action. You need to remember that doesn't matter what type of environment that you have been living in you need to give yourself proper time to think about the things that have been making you angry. If you don't give the proper thought about the exact event that actually has been making you really mad and agree and also frustrated at the same time then obviously you will not be able to get over it. Because running from it has never been an option and it never will be.

Anger management workbook for men

CHAPTER 6: HANDLING FACTS AND TAKING THE SUPPRESSION TO THE NEXT LEVEL

I don't even need you to teach you about the basic principles of perspective. As you have been reading this book to learn more about anchor management and you probably have been giving a lot of time for yourself to come yourself down in an efficient way. You already know that how you are looking at things makes all the difference.

Let me give you a comparatively easy story to listen and also to understand about the facts. In the last chapter I told you about a story regarding my project and how I have been able to get less scores that I was truly capable of just because that I was frustrated about something that didn't make any sense and also not any change. You could easily notice that the way that I was looking at the intersection was totally wrong. And it is also true that, at the moment of my action I was not being able to notice the fact. As I have given a lot of time to myself in the thought of why I have been so angry and how well I could have performed by using just a different perspective inside my head, a whole new world of opportunities was opened right in front of me.

I knew very well that doesn't matter how I am reacting or how I am thinking about a specific matter, there's always another way around. Even the most obvious thing has at least two or three different ways of seeing it. This is the only thing that I failed to understand. and also this is the only thing that most of the people fail

Anger management workbook for men

to understand regularly. I know that, As I'm telling you that you need to change your perspective, This will obviously not make any actual change inside your personality. And that is why I would not tell you that you must change your perspective about different things and you need to see things differently that you have been already. I will do a simple task. All I will do is I will explain the opportunities and the benefits that you are going to be having if you have been able to change your perspective. You will automatically feel motivated to think more and other way around regarding the same situation that you have been facing every single day of your life.

Let me give you the simplest and the most convenient example ever. In our daily life the thing that we use every single day is food. There are some gross people that might not even brush their teeth regularly. There are some people that have the habit of living on a dirty environment and they don't even shower regularly. But food is something that none of us is able to avoid. To be honest, If you think about it in this way, food is the only thing that we do all the works in our life. From studying 10 to 20 years of our life to working 9 to 5 hours of our work day and earning a lot of money and working day and night just to make our lives a better place is only for the purpose of getting the food first. Imagine that you have only a couple of sense inside your wallet. The first thought that will come inside your mind is that how are you going to be able to eat this evening? I'm not saying that only the thought of food is going to be inside your head. But that is obviously going to be the first thing that you will be thinking. Whatever you are out at your shopping or doing your groceries, If you live in the middle Eastern or the southern Asian countries or even if you have the idea about such stuff of countries then you know that the supermall or the super shop type of concept such as

Anger management workbook for men

Walmart or similar other stores are not quite popular in those countries. People usually bargain for the price for even the slightest thing that they have to buy. If you have seen in a middle Eastern or Indian movies and that movie has a scene of market, you already know that people and especially women do a lot of bargaining whenever they are buying something. This whole culture of bargaining for the price might not be quite the culture in the Western countries such as the United States or the European countries. But that doesn't mean that Western people don't bargain for price. Every single business deal or every single deal of purchasing a property requires a lot of bargaining and a lot of negotiation in terms of getting up to a proper and healthy price. Let me tell you the entire story with both the mixed perspective of the Asian Eastern and the western concept. Imagine that you are purchasing a property to build your house. The previous owner of the property has asked for $50,000 from you for the price of the land. But you know very well that if you really want to efficiently build the infrastructure that you want to make at that place, Which the entire budget of making the whole building you need to be able to bring the price down up to $35,000. In this case you will be trying your best to bring the amount of price down as close as possible to $35,000. Whenever you are not being able to get lower than 40,000 dollars and you still have to buy the property you will be under a lot of frustration. The frustration is true and also rational. But think about the entire situation like this, If that piece of land is the only suitable property that is going to be perfect for your business or the house that you are willing to build, then it is obviously a reasonable price to give. Whenever you're not being able to reach the exact same goal that you wish to achieve, you need to think in this way that things could have been worse. This single little sentence that " things could have been worse" would change your entire life.

Anger management workbook for men

There is maybe the very first lesson that you need to learn about changing your perspective towards things. Because the way that we are thinking about things around us changes everything that we ever know. I know that if I am talking about prospective and how you are thinking about different things around you it might sound way too much obvious. But the problem is that, As we know that the method in front of us is really obvious and childish we tend to give very little attention towards it. And while thinking about how the fact is really obvious and it is just not that much important we forget to even follow that simple little thing. What I'm trying to say is that, Whenever we are thinking that this method is too easy to follow we don't even try that because we think that something this much easy might not be able to give us the proper result that we have been searching for. And just because of that we are really less likely to follow any type of method that seems really easy or achievable to us.

Let me tell you another story about how perspective will help you changing your life. Imagine that you are working in a corporate sector related company. Obviously, The company that you are going to be working in will have a lot of busy movements and also there are going to be a lot of instructions to follow. At the same time, You are going to be having a lot of arguments and a lot of heated conversation with your superior officer. and add first type of stage it is very much possible that you are going to be way too much frustrated and angry with the behavior of your superior correspondent of the company. I am not telling you that being angry is really irrelevant at this point because of that your officer in charge has shouted at you. But what I'm trying to say is that if you are thinking about it like this, Even your superior officer has to answer toward someone and he also is under a lot of stress. Just to maintain the proper service from the

Anger management workbook for men

employees working under him, and to maintain the proper impression with his superior officers, he will be under a lot of stress and also a lot of pressure in terms of maintaining the proper productivity of the company. He might be just shouting at you out of his dress or frustration. I'm not justifying that you should be yelled at all times. But what I'm trying to say is that if you are getting angry just because of your superior has shouted at you, The same might be happening to the other person at the same time as well. When you start to think about different situations in front of you like this, you will automatically notice that you are getting less angry and also you are staying calm down for the most part. This is exactly what I'm trying to say. learn to think and see things from the different perspective. it doesn't matter how much he did the situation is or how much he did the conversation is that you are going through, unsetting fast or within just under a couple of seconds will not give you any other results and what you are having right now. If unsetting fast is not giving you any extra results then why should you bother? Just take your time for even a couple of seconds to reply to something right after you have heard it. That extra two or second of time that you were taking before replying to someone in a heated argument will make all the difference between how much you are able to hold up your mood and also how much you are able to handle the entire situation in a suitable way.

Anger management workbook for men

CHAPTER 7: SHIFTING FOCUS TO MANAGE ANGER EVEN BETTER

In this chapter we are going to be learning about how to shift your focus towards the facts rather than what is actually happening in front of you. The situation is mostly used for whenever another person is really angry at you and also his situation is making you mad at him at the same time. Let me give you a small demonstration on explanation to a story. Imagine that you and I we both are close friends and we are talking in front of each other. That is certain point of our conversation we slowly start to turn towards some controversial things in which we both have opposing thoughts. for obvious reasons we are going to be talking in the exact opposite direction from one another and also we will be giving opinions on a certain fact totally different from one another. This step of situation has a large compatibility and potential of creating a heated argument between us. Imagine that, In this heart and point of our conversation you said something regarding a fact that is sensitive to me. But what you said about that fact is totally wrong and something that I would not like under any circumstances. At this moment it is very much possible that I will start yelling back at you. But the thing is that whenever I'm yelling back at you and I'm mad just as you as you are on me, I'm not being able to see a simple fact. it can be very much possible that the sentence that you have just said regarding that specific fact has something to do with your past life and you are really disturbed by it on a personal manner. But the thing is that whenever I am shouting back at you as soon as you are shouting at me it is very much possible that I will not be able to understand the

Anger management workbook for men

perspective behind why and how you are saying that speech towards me. If I had taken just a couple of seconds before replying towards your speech I would have understood that why were you speaking such type of facts in front of me. Everything happens for a reason in this world. But people are so much rushed and so much in a face that we often do not give enough time to understand why something is happening right in front of us. All we see is that something is happening in front of us and we start acting towards it as soon as possible. We do not give ourselves the time to understand that if we have taken a couple of seconds at least just to think about it before we say it out loud, things could have been totally different.

Whenever a situation is in front of you that another person or the situation itself has been presenting itself towards you with a heated characteristics, The first tendency that you should have in your mind is not to respond. The first tendency that you should have in your mind is to look for the fact upon which the situation is happening in front of you. We all have suffered with a bad roommate in our hostel life. We might have stayed to suspect roommates that are annoyed and pissed off all the time at something. obviously we are annoyed by the disturbance of that person because he is mad and pissed off and shouting all the time. But it is also true that we have not given a single try to understand why that person is shouting that much. Just by saying a couple of comforting words to that person we might be able to make his or her day. If we focus on the facts upon which that person is behaving rashly, We can easily be able to make ourselves capable of understanding why everything is happening in front of us and also we can come up with a better alternative approach rather than just yelling out. Imagine that you are just chilling in your room listening to music or maybe having a little study over your next

Anger management workbook for men

weekend exam, at this moment your roommate rushes into your room yelling out about everything that how much he is really mad at a specific guy and so on. Obviously the entire silence of your room is going to be shattered into a million pieces. And also it is very much possible that you were going to be pissed off at your roommate at the same time. Most of the arguments between roommates tend to happen in such type of moments. I'm not saying that your silence or the peace that you were enjoying doesn't have any value. But there are some situations and circumstances where it doesn't matter how much we are enjoying ourselves our privacy doesn't matter that much in comparison with the need of the other person in front of us. instead of just yelling out at your roommate back about how he has been ruining your entire mood and how he has been joining the entire environment of the room, Just ask him how is he doing and why is he so stressed out. It is very much possible that he's going to be repeating the same things over and over again for a couple of time. But all will be quickly silent after a short time. This is what I've been trying to explain to you. instead of just getting back at your roommate you could just simply take a couple of seconds to understand why he is behaving like that. You need to be able to train yourself and also keeping your mind that whenever a situation or a circumstance is right in front of you, you need to be able to look at the facts first and react later.

Now, I'm going to be telling you a little more about why focusing up on facts is really important.

Focusing upon facts instead of just yelling out in front of the other person is also really very helpful in terms of maintaining family relationships. The thing is that, people are more likely to let go of all their frustration in front of a family member. I'm not telling that you

Anger management workbook for men

shouldn't estimate the strength of the relationship between two family members. But what I'm trying to basically say is that despite the other person is your family member but he still or she still is an individual human being. With individual taste and individual mood swings and also individual circumstances that he or she might be going to at that moment. it is very much possible that despite of he or she is a close family member to you, whenever you are letting go eat a frustration in that moment it might be very much possible that the other person might not be in the position to take whatever you are saying. The same thing is possible even if it is working the other way around. But the thing is that whenever family member are ideal friends to you is talking to you about how he's been frustrated or even because of his frustrated by something else he's letting all of those frustration on to you, I know that it is really obvious to feel bad or sometimes even feel angry at that person because you are getting yelled at without even doing anything. And of course, why should you be get shouted at this bit of the fact that you didn't even do anything and it has nothing to do with you? The fun part about human communication and our society is that doesn't matter what we are liking and what we are not we need to be putting our focus on what is right and what is wrong. If your reacting towards something really irrational happening with you brings no benefit for you then why should you waste your effort in doing it? Imagine that your wife all your husband has come home from work and he or she is really frustrating and yelling at you for even the slightest mistake and you know that you're getting childhood absolutely no reason and it is very much possible that you are getting shouted at because of someone else's mistake. And that situation is really very possible for you to be equally angry at the other person in front of you. But if you are just able to hold your anger for

Anger management workbook for men

that moment it won't do any harm. People do a simple mistake in this case and that is, Whenever the other person is doing something irrational and getting angry, They do not stand to shout back at them and they just simply hold the anger and don't express how they have been feeling regarding this. The problem is that this amount of anger and is amount of negative feeling towards the other person is going to get stored inside your brain and also it is very much true that at some point it is going to all come out at once. This might be the reason behind so many breakups of relationships and also the higher amount of ratio for divorce between couples. This is all happening because we either express ourselves way too much or we don't express ourselves at all. Most of the time we are actually failing to realize what is the exact and the most perfect amount to express ourselves and when is the correct time. If I am angry at you, And I just don't yell at you because I don't want any argument or any type of heated conversation among us, at some point it is all going to be coming out. And for the reason that it is all going to be coming out is going to be something so much irrelevant and so much small that even I am going to be quite shocked that how is such type of a small event capable of it ruining the entire relationship.

What should be done here is that, instead of just yelling back at you right at the moment whenever you're reacting to me I should be quiet for the moment. And after a certain number of time when you are calm down and also you are ready to hear to my reasoning and explanation, I can easily tell you by just saying that I felt really bad regarding how you reacted towards me in that previous time. If I get the feeling that if I tell you this in this manner then you might be angry again then I can easily tell you that, "hey I actually felt really bad about how you reacted towards me previously, But I really want

Anger management workbook for men

to know what happened to you and what made you so angry if you could share to me it would be better for me to understand and also I could be able to help you".

Just in the previous quotation I have shown you that how you can exactly express that you have felt really bad by the behavior of the other person and also you have given them a sense of comfort that they will automatically start to feel guilty inside them. It's just like getting a double kill. You also are able to make the other person feel exactly how you wanted when you were angry and you still were able to give him the sense of comfort that you were someone dear to him. This will make the person truly understand about what type of mistake that they have done and also he or she will be more open towards you and also more helpful towards you in future incidents.

Anger management workbook for men

CHAPTER 8: SOLVING THINGS ONE AT A TIME

I know that this book has not been your typical how to do and what to do to solve that problem. I also know that I am not just giving you out random tips and tricks on how to get your anger down in just 30 days. But if you have been reading this book till now with a proper amount of focus then you already know a lot about anger and how it could be managed. anger management is a sensitive thing to do inside any personality because it is not something that can be bound by a fixed set of rules. of course there might be a common pattern or maybe a couple of common patterns to follow in order to properly calm yourself down. But the real thing is that every person is unique on his or her individual existence. And if you really want yourself to get ahead of this problem and solve it as soon as possible and also that solution is sustainable then you need to learn the step by step process. The step by step process learning might not be able to just give you a clear vision about how you can come yourself down or how you can be 100% successful at your anger management. But it will give you the ability to understand the problem and also come up with proper solutions by yourself so that you don't need help of anyone else or you don't need to be waiting for the entire process to work for you. The main purpose or the main goal of this book for which I have written this book is only because I want you to be able to understand the entire situation and also to utilize every single element on your favor to turn the table.

Anger management workbook for men

I know that I have been wasting a lot of time in this chapter of just speaking about how you can make yourself better rather than just talking about the actual information itself. I truly apologize for that and also without wasting the time we are going to be jumping right into the subject matter of this chapter.

This chapter is all about how you can take the proper responsibility for something that you have done. I know that there are sometimes that something that you might have done is not actually your fault or it might have been caused because some incident or action taken by someone else. But the person that is judging you by the work that you have done is not going to be considering the fact whether or not someone else has made you into their own puppet and made you do the bad thing. The truth is that despite of being total logical that if it is caused because of someone else it doesn't matter whether or not you have done it, that is not how the practical world works for the most part. it has been most possible that something or some wrongdoings that has been done might be in existence to only because of someone else's fault. For say we can say that, you are walking on the street with a coffee cup on your hand that you have just gotten from the coffee shop, and suddenly your legs slip on something that has been left by some other passerby. It is very much true that you absolutely did not have any responsibility in terms of the existence of the event. But when you slept on the road, your coffee cup was tossed and the entire coffee was on someone else's dress. it is obviously your moral duty to apologize to that person. Doesn't matter for which cause the incident has occurred. All that matters and all that you need to keep in your mind that if the acting person is you on the first hand then you should be taking the responsibility before anyone else. Doesn't matter if it is rational or not it is what needs to be done. I know that

Anger management workbook for men

sometimes it might not seem logical or even it might not seem fair to you. But this is something that will help you maintain a proper balance of your environment and also the vibe that you will be having from other people around you. Even if you think all of these as really irrational and really illogical to do, think of the intern situation like this. If something illogical can bring you the biggest and harmony in your personal life that something logical never has been able to do, then what is the downside of doing the illogical thing? After all, peace is all that we seek in our life. If something that we really don't appreciate that much gives us the peace in our life that we truly seek, then it is obviously better for us to get used to it as soon as possible. That is from a totally neutral perspective in which you have no other way but to just accept it. But that is not the way of totally accepting something. Taking responsibility and not only makes you a humble person inside the mind of the person in front of you, but also it will make you capable to understand how you can change the world just by taking responsibility for something that you have done.

When you are used to taking responsibilities for everything that you have done you will automatically start to develop a sense of security that doesn't matter whatever you are doing you have to take responsibility and for that you will be more prone towards making things perfect and also less careless. When you have the habit of taking responsibility for everything that you have done, You will automatically start to have the intention inside your mind to make the thing right in the first place. Not just the intention or the psychological condition that you're having inside your mind, there are other perks to it too. I know that this might sound a lot childish and also naïve, But when you have a personality that you take responsibility for all the right and all the wrong things that

Anger management workbook for men

you have done you will automatically start to have a sense of comfort and also confidence in your personality. You will start to feel the control of your life that you have and also you will start to have a better trip of the things that you are about to do or you're giving effort to do.

You might have a question that what does all these have to do with anger management? is because when you are much more confident with your own life and also confident about every single action that you are doing, you will be able to see things differently and also from a responsible perspective that you will have a sense automatically developed inside you. The sense that I am talking about is going to give you the capability of looking at things differently. Not only the perspective, But also you will be totally able to handle things with a much more calmed down mind. The feeling and the sense of responsibility does this much better to you.

Anger management workbook for men

CHAPTER 9: DISCUSSION ON ANGER TRIGGERS

In the previous chapters, I have told you about how you can change your anger trigger by just thinking about something the other way around. The reason is that whenever you are putting your perspective towards a specific object in a certain way it is very much possible that you will be blocking any other perspective or any other meaning of the same event. This might occur quite a lot among most of the people because whenever we are in an intense situation, it is not quite possible that we will be thinking about different perspectives in the first place. The first thing that will be basically coming inside your mind is how you can react towards the situation and how you can tell the other person that has done something wrong about what type of mistake that he has done. This might be one of the most common reaction or one of the most common impulses of a natural human being. But the thing is that doesn't mean it is going to be good if it is natural. eating a lot of food that has been freshly grown over trees doesn't necessarily mean that you will be having a good health by it. Imagine that you have diabetes. Apple is obviously one of the most juiciest and fresh fruits that are growing around us all the time. If you eat a lot of apple which is full with sugar and also a lot of items that is not friendly with a patient who has been suffering with diabetes, it will obviously never mean that you will be having good health or any type of other benefits by doing so. That is the exact one that I've been trying to explain to you throughout this entire book. something being a natural doesn't necessarily mean that it will be good for you or for the people around you. And that is exactly why

Anger management workbook for men

I'm going to management and giving proper attention towards angry management is really important for us to maintain the proper balance and peace and also the harmony of our social life. I'm not telling you that the events that have occurred in front of you or even some annoying behavior done by someone else in front of you is not worth of being angry. I'm also not telling you that if you are getting angry by some work done by another person in front of you it is really bad that you are acting in such way. But the thing is that if acting naturally brings you nothing but harm and imbalance in your social life then why should you bother? The first thing that you must try to learn and understand is the proper value of yourself and the proper value of the mode that you have. Maybe only in this case, I'm going to be telling you that you need to be selfish. If your selfish about how you are behaving or how you are feeling about something and if you are selfish about giving value towards your mood, you will be easily able to understand that reacting to everything that is bad happening in front of you is not totally worth it. It is obviously not totally worth it regarding the time or even the mode that you will be losing by reacting toward something.

That is why in this chapter I will be telling about how you can observe your thoughts and also give yourself proper time on just thinking about how you are thinking about different situations and different perspectives. Whenever you are giving yourself a lot of time just for thinking about the reactions that you have been giving out in the past towards different situation you will be able to understand a lot of things newly about yourself. more than 90% of the people usually think that giving yourself proper time and also just imagining everything that you have done and how you have been reacting towards it, is

Anger management workbook for men

totally lame and also not worth it. But let me give you an explanatory story to understand.

Think about yourself in this case. Imagine that you are a typical middle-aged man with a 9 to 5 job and also a happy family. One of your neighbors who is really prone towards listening to loud music disregarding the comfort of the person or the people surrounding his neighborhood, has a common tendency towards blasting out loud heavy metal music at the middle of the night. This will obviously be capable of making you way too much angry. Because the entire piece and harmony of the society is going to be hampered and also you are going to be losing a lot of your good nights sleep. But imagine that you are getting angry and yelling and even threatening him to sue if he doesn't turn down the volume of the music. Before actually reacting it in such type of impulsive manner you need to understand the perspective about the person. If the person was so much reasonable and so much rational in terms of thinking about how other people might be affected by his behavior he would not have done this in the first place. That basically means that, Even if you are threatening to even assault him on a physical basis it will have absolutely zero impact on the entire situation. On the downside, you will be losing a lot of your temper and also the anger is going to be causing a lot of high blood pressure inside you which is obviously not good for your mental and also physical health conditions. Now tell me that, does yelling really help? Does this make anything better than it already is?

The answer towards both of the previous question is obviously no. So what could you do in this point? You could gather a lot of the neighbors around your society and for force him to stop the music. Or even there is a better way, instead of just yelling out at him you could

Anger management workbook for men

simply call the police on him. That should teach him a lesson. Have you noticed that yelling and just shouting and losing a lot of your temper didn't get the thing that you want. Whenever you stop to think about that person and how that person is actually thinking about the entire situation helped you a lot in terms of holding both your anger and also maintaining the inner peace that you have. This is exactly how you can change a lot of things happening around you and your reaction towards them just by observing your thoughts.

Because it is really normal to shout out with anger in terms of such type of occurrence. But whenever you gave a little bit of time towards yourself to think about the entire situation and how you have been thinking about it totally made all the changes.

I do realize that there are going to be some certain situations which will be able to trigger you so much that you will not be able to come yourself down under any circumstances. Apart from the really exceptional situations, you could easily just give yourself a little bit of time even that time is for a couple of seconds to think about the intern situation and how you can get more efficiency in terms of getting out the result for the thing that you are wanting to happen.

Let's talk about how you can calm down yourself totally just by choosing the proper words whenever even you are thinking about a situation.

Have you ever noticed that whenever you're thinking about something it is almost like a movie happening inside your brain. You imagine all the scenes and all the characters in front of you having a discussion

Anger management workbook for men

and even the words just flow through your mind like movie dialogues. But the thing is that whenever we are thinking we might think that a situation or a person that has really annoyed us up to a certain level, it is quite reasonable to get angry from the inside and stay calmed down on the exterior level. One of the common tendency of most of the people who are really prone towards getting angry whenever anything annoying is happening in front of them is that, We like to think in such a way "Doesn't matter whatever I am thinking from the inside I will be polite on the outside and be gentle towards the person who is making me angry."

That does not solve anything. Just like I told you in the previous chapters that whenever you're trying to suppress your angers it is not going to be going anywhere rather than it is going to be staying in the same place in your mind and also at some point it is going to be coming out bursting. Such type of a situation is more likely to make you the bad person. Because imagine that I am a person that has been annoying you for a lot of time. I might have done really big mistakes in front of you and also made you really angry but you were not expressing your anger rather than you were just suppressing the entire emotion inside you. At some day I accidentally drop a glass of water and break the glass. At that point, it is very much possible that you will be lashing out with all of your angers that you have been storing inside yourself for me. It is true that you have a lot of anger regarding the behavior that I have been doing for such a long time. But if you think about this inter situation from a third person perspective, what would you see?

You will see that the person in front of you has just yelled and shouted in really in and in human way just because the other person broke a glass. Don't think about

Anger management workbook for men

yourself, think about me in the place instead. Imagine that you are in front of me and I am just yelling really inhumanely at someone because that person has broken a glass.

You will be quite disgusted by the personality that I have. But obviously you will not be able to actually realize the amount of anger that I have stored inside myself for that person's past behavior. That is exactly what I'm trying to tell you.

Whenever we are getting angry and we are thinking about the intern situation inside our mind it is very much possible that we will be thinking in an angry perspective. But it is really important to even choose the words correctly whenever we are thinking about a specific situation. Most of the people who have been giving a lot of efforts for anger management failed at this point. Because this part of being polite on the outside they store and even think in an angry manner. This doesn't actually help in any way. Let me give you a little bit of story from my personal life again to elaborate the entire explanation.

I'm going to be referring towards my student life again. There was a guy named Rogers. I'm not going to be mentioning his full name due to privacy concerns. So this Rogers guy, he was in the same class at me and also he had the same major course. Which basically means that I will be seeing him for the most of the time of my college life. The problem is that he was really a dirty and ugly guy. I'm not telling him ugly by the reference of how he looks on his face. I'm telling him ugly because he's really a bad and mean and such rude person from the inside. He was bullying all the other innocent students in the class and also harassing a lot of the girls. it was quite possible for me to just simply lash out at him with anger and even go on all physical in an attempt to slow him down. But I

Anger management workbook for men

couldn't do that. Because he was almost as twice as high and also as twice as wide than me. Even if I yelled at him, a simple punch would have knocked me down for the weekend. And I know that the type of person that he is, explaining and persuading him into understanding the situation that being so mean and rude has no meaning and it is only making him a bad person is totally useless. I was in such a state that I was neither in the position of protesting or even making the situation of the class better in any way. But I was getting quite stressed from the inside because whenever the thought of getting into that class was coming inside my mind the first thing that was popping out in front of my eyes was his face. And whenever that was happening, I was getting angry from the inside. Even if he was in front of me I was behaving quite politely and I was thinking really angry from my inside. This was getting me absolutely nowhere. Because this was creating the entire situation inside my psychological world just in the way as I have just yelled at him for a couple of hours. Which means that being angry from the inside and polite from the outside doesn't actually get the thing that you want. In fact, it does quite the opposite.

There was a certain time that I was so much stressed out that I even thought about leaving the inter class and joining some other course. But slowly as the time flew by, I started to think about myself. about how I have been so much angry from the inside and it is getting me absolutely nowhere. I even thought a couple of time that I should just lash out at him. But the inner reasoning compatibility of my mind kept on stopping me from doing that. After a certain amount of time I realized that I was able to ignore him totally even from my inside and also from the thoughts of my subconscious mind. Then I realized that, If I was thinking about his entire situation

Anger management workbook for men

about how much a rude and mean person he is, and thinking about him and how I could stop him is absolutely getting me nowhere. It was giving me a lot of peace. Because whenever I was able to realize from my inside that thinking about him was making me have absolutely nothing but just wasting a lot of my personal time and inner peace of my mind, it gave me the power to ignore him on the ultimate way. I mean, like seriously. From the inside, I was able to achieve a state of mind in such a way that he didn't even exist in my world. This made my world totally simple and full of peace again.

That is why observing your thoughts and also shaping how you have been choosing your words inside your mind in terms of thinking about a specific situation has an important role to play in terms of getting your anger management into a proper structure.

That is basically all for this chapter. At this point of this book, I will be discussing about how you can take criticism about yourself coming out from the person in front of you and also control your responses regarding that criticism at the same time.

If somehow, you still haven't lost the interest of reading this book by the boring and dumb explanations that I have been giving you, congratulations.

All I have to say to you about all these is that, boring or not, the things that I've been telling you in this book will definitely be able to help you to think clearer and also in such a way that will be helpful for both living a balanced life and also a peaceful one.

Anger management workbook for men

CHAPTER 10: MANAGING CRITICISM

In the chapter we will be talking about everything regarding criticism and how you can manage your responses towards it. The fun thing about criticism is that, In most of the common cases happening around us all the time we feel the necessity to react impulsively whenever we are being criticized about something that we have done. The reason behind reacting so impulsively in terms of taking criticism regarding something that we have been doing for a lot of time and also we have put a lot of effort into it is that there is a certain amount of personal attachment along with a lot of time that we have invested into it for making it happen. Imagine the entire scenario like this, You have been walking on a project for your high school regarding how the environment can be changed in the good way by just making some simple changes. You have been thinking a lot about this entire project for months after months. And also you have given hours of restless nights from your life to create that beautiful little model with Styrofoam. now imagine that whenever you're taking that project to school one of your neighbors just caught you at your doorstep. as your neighbor was looking on to your project she suddenly noticed that you didn't do quite well without lines and it all looks just childish and gibberish. Despite all the fact that I've been in of that woman might be 100% true but still you are going to be reacting out quite impulsively. The reason is that you have been spending a lot of time and also you have sacrificed a lot of your sleep in terms of making it happen. But whenever someone is criticizing you on the interfered that you have been given into that project in such manner you

Anger management workbook for men

will be obviously getting a lot of anger build up inside your brain.

You might be asking at this point that, If someone does that type of criticism towards something that you have loved and given so much effort into, then how on God's earth are you not supposed to be angry at them?

The thing is that, is not unnatural or irrational to be angry at that point. But you need to be thinking about yourself and your mood at the first place. Just like I told you in the previous chapter, You need to be prioritizing yourself before anyone else. Prioritize yourself in numero uno, and then everyone else. Numero uno means number one in Spanish. Just for the sake of clarification. Whenever you're giving proper priority towards your efforts and also the time that you have been investing into something then you will be automatically able to give yourself the proper value and care less about what others have to say about you. One of the old proverb in the English literature is that keep your friends close and your enemies closer. The reason behind this speech is that whenever you're keeping someone that hates you from the bottom of their heart at a close range you will be able to observe how they have been reacting towards your success. The fun part is that, people who usually despise you, are going to be quite attentive towards your work for finding out even the smallest mistakes. This actually has a lot of benefits if you think about it in this way. Because whenever you're giving so much effort and so much time and so much hard working to making something happen it is very much possible that small details might be overlooked by you. The people who despise you the most will be the easiest way to get to know about the mistakes that you have left behind unnoticed. Don't think about the people who have been criticizing you as someone bad. Think about them as

Anger management workbook for men

a method are a media to learn more about what type of mistakes that you are doing. Don't take the criticism as your inter work is ruined and it is not off any value. Take the criticism in such a way inside your mind, that you should be able to realize what type of small mistakes that you have overlooked into the project.

I do realize that whenever someone in front of us is giving a lot of effort into making something happen the ideal approach towards him or her should be to appreciate the efforts and the achievement that they have got. Not just criticize the hell out of them about what type of mistakes that they have left behind. This is the ideal approach actually. Because in a perfect world we would be thinking about how that person has been giving a lot of effort and he should be appreciated in a certain way. But the reality is that, Not even 10% of the population think about everything in this way. If people used to think in the ideal way then the world should not have been such a massacre. Back to the point which I was explaining. Whenever someone is criticizing you, it doesn't mean that you should just be angry at them because they are not valuing the effort or the work that you have done. it is because you should be happy that there are a certain amount of people that are attentive towards your work and they are pointing out your mistakes on behalf of you. If someone does a critical work on behalf of you then would you be mad at them or would you be just happy that someone else is doing your work?

Finding out or pointing out the mistakes on your own work is maybe the hardest thing ever to do in this world. Because whenever we are giving effort and focus on to something, it is very common that we might understand some small mistakes or errors that might leave a big impact on the end product. And this critical

Anger management workbook for men

part of the entire world is done by someone else. Then why should you be mad at them? Despite all the fact that the tone of speaking while criticizing you might not be quite as much pleasing as you hope for it to be.

Now let me give you the proper structure about what I'm explaining you. You imagine that you and me, We are in front of each other. And I have just shown you one of the biggest projects of my entire life. When you are watching my project and seeing everything that I have done you are finding out small mistakes that I have left behind. But I was actually hoping that you would appreciate how much good work that I have done and I was hoping for a conversation from you that I have achieved this much. But whenever you are criticizing me on the smallest mistake in the first place rather than just appreciating me for that you meant that I have got, it is very much obvious for me to get mad at you even from the inside because I am not getting the proper appreciation or I am getting rejection from you in that place where I was supposed to be getting a lot of congratulations.

If I am getting mad at you and I'm being angry at the entire fact it is very much possible that I, myself, am going to be losing a lot of focus from the project itself. The entire enthusiasm that I had inside my mind regarding the entire work would be gone into ruins. That is scenario number one.

But what if instead of getting mad, I'm thinking about dentist you like this. Because of spending a lot of time I was quite stressed and frustrated regarding the whole project and I was not being able to put a lot of focus on to what I have already done. This made me overlook and sometimes miss a lot of mistakes that I've left behind in the project. While you are criticizing me, I am also being able to learn about even the smallest mistake that I have

Anger management workbook for men

left behind. And by this way, I'm able to actually make my work as close as perfection that it is possible for me to be. Now tell me. Which one is better?

You already know the answer.

Anger management workbook for men

CHAPTER 11: CRITICISM (MORE)

Before even starting with the main subject matter of the chapter I need to do something to you. The entire object that is going to be discussed in this chapter is related with the previous chapter about taking criticism. In the previous after I told you about how you can change your perspective towards when you have been criticized. But in this afternoon I will be discussing about how you can control your response and exactly in which way you can achieve the success in terms of giving out proper response as whenever you are being criticized or under a lot of stress. Because in the last chapter, I only told you about how you can change your perspective regarding whenever you are being criticized about something. But whenever you are changing your perspective towards it it is very much possible that you will still have a little bit of impulse inside you. Whenever you are getting criticized it is very much possible that you will still be angry because your effort and your hard work is not going to be appreciated as much as you have wanted it to be.

In the chapter we will be discussing about how you can control your responses and also what will be the ideal exercise for making your response schedule in a proper manner.

You need to follow some simple psychological exercises inside your brain on a regular basis. If you are able to find a suitable amount of time of at least 30 minutes every day, And if you're not able to give 30 minutes of time in this exercise every day then just take

Anger management workbook for men

the weekends and spend at least 30 minutes. The exercise that you are going to be doing is going to be as follows:

You need to sit down in a calm and quiet place. If you have any room in your house that is usually not used frequently then that is going to be the ideal place for it. And if you don't have a room then just pick an ideal time of the day in which the other members of your family or the other members living in the same house are not going to be quite physically as active as the usually be in the other times of the day. When you have got the proper place and the proper time, now you need to set up the proper environment. There are some traditional books based on community behavioral therapy and also guided meditation that will tell you to find an ambient lightened room along with some soft music to play on the background and so on. But I'm going to do a telling you that just go for whatever makes you comfortable. Even if you were comfortable with having metal music being played on the background and just do it. It's simple. Just go over the environment that is most comfortable to you. At the situation try to set on the exact middle of the room where you have a lot of space on every side of your body. sit inside of a place in which you have a lot of air flow and also that air is fresh. Not that you have said your proper environment start thinking about the incidence and start thinking about the past occurrences in which you have been angry. Imagine yourself as the main character of a movie and imagine the entire scenario as the movie itself happening all around you. Try to relive every single moment once again. I do realize that reliving some angry moments of your past life might be able to trigger a lot of anxiety and also a lot of frustration inside you again. But don't try to fight it. Tried to face it. Not all of the problems in our lives should be faced in such manner. But if there is one problem in our internal lifetime that should be faced

Anger management workbook for men

head on then that is this. Now when you have already said down the proper environment and also the proper place and time of the day start thinking about the events as it is happening right in front of you right now.

At this moment when you are going through the same moments over and over again, Try to look for all the approaches rather than just lashing out with anger. Try to look and keep looking for the best alternative way until you have found one. And when you do, imagine the internal with that alternative method again. I've already bringing in any of the angry moments inside this last moment. Now you will have a basic and ideal idea about what should be the proper approach in terms of getting in touch with such type of circumstance again. This would be able to help you in terms of getting a proper structure in front of you regarding what type of response should be ideal whenever you are facing the similar event once again. But you might ask that this is just one type of circumstances. What about the others? That is exactly why I have been telling you to give this exercise a sufficient amount of time on a regular basis. If you can do it daily then great. If you can't do it daily then find a suitable day or is suitable time from the entire week. Whatever the fact or what about the time it is you need to be maintaining a proper and regular exercise in terms of doing this again and again. After only a couple of months you will be able to realize that you have changed a lot. Because thinking to ourselves and also talking to ourselves as maybe the action that is done leased by the people but should be done the most.

And when you combine this exercise with all of the other methods and all of the other perspective changing speeches that I have been giving you throughout this entire book you will be able to have a lot of

Anger management workbook for men

clarifications about what I've been telling you. Whenever you are exercising like this on a regular basis and also you are keeping in mind about all the perspectives and all the theories that I have told you and explain to you throughout this entire book You will automatically realize that within just a couple of months you are able to change yourself a lot in the good way.

Anger management workbook for men

CHAPTER 12: MIND GAME

If you have been around the internet researching about how you can get your anger into a proper management system then you already have come across a lot of medication and such type of psychological or therapeutic programs. If you just simply Google what you are looking for then you are going to have a lot of medication and such type of suggestions for medical treatments for anger management and some type of little programs. I'm not saying that medical procedure or professional medication is not good for you neither am I claiming that such type of procedure or elements are totally useless.

But the thing is that, In most of the cases that are related to psychological or any type of personality related issues it is proof and that if you are depending too much on any type of medication or any type of other certified medicine then you are going to be totally getting dependent onto that. What would you prefer more? Have a more sustainable result or just keep depending on the medications?

The medications are the professional and formal medical treatment might be able to reduce your anger related issues up to a certain level. But that type of solution is never sustainable neither anyone can claim the guarantee of its being sustainable up to a certain level.

If you really want a true and sustainable solution towards such type of serious and critical problem of your personality then you need to follow the entire process of anger management and also the most important thing that

Anger management workbook for men

you need to do is to give yourself proper time to understand the circumstances and come up with best alternative reactions and responses by yourself.

Meditation might be the best answer towards all of your problems. a lot of people that actually think that meditation and such type of other spiritual activities to cleanse your mind and soul are totally bogus and it is nothing but just a hoax of the internet.

The thing is that if you really want to know about the truth of meditation and self type of other methods then you really need to do an in-depth study about it. In this chapter I will not be able to discuss the entire details about meditation and exactly how you can get benefited from it. But that is not what I am trying to do here. What I'm basically trying to do in this chapter is to explain you what meditation is and how it is actually going to be able to make your situation better than before. And also in this chapter, I will be giving you a scientific explanation and also the proper understanding about how meditation actually works to make yourself better.

If you are a a person that likes a proper explanation towards everything that is happening around you then you will be quiet willing to understand the science end of principles behind your meditation and how it has been able to change the life of millions of people.

The basic policy of meditation and the whole perspective behind it is to create your body and your mind in such a way that it is going to be able to find a peaceful state at all times. imagine when you are anxious or even when you are stressed or frustrated about something it is very obvious that your brain is going to be reducing a lot of the good hormones that control the good mode of your personality. That is due to the fact that whenever we are

Anger management workbook for men

anxious or frustrated or any other type of negative emotion is consuming us our brain starts to release some different and specific type of hormones that controls our reaction and also our psychological state of mind. The main purpose of meditation is to create the psychological stress free environment inside your brain in such a way that you are able to reduce the negative hormones inside your body and also increase the positive and soothing hormones inside your blood stream so that you are able to think better and also you are able to have a peace of your mind.

I'm not dealing that you should never take meditation for any type of anger management related issues. What I'm trying to say is that, You should really feel the necessity to do it, big proper gardens from certified physician and then take medications to reduce the situation that is already happening with you. But you need to keep in your mind at all times that doesn't matter what type of medicine that you are taking you cannot be totally dependent on it. Because if you are, That is going to be a certain time when you will not have your medicines near your reach and also you will be having an anger outburst. And that situation the type of circumstance that you are going to be facing and also the angular issues that you are going to be facing is absolutely something that you don't want to do.

And that is exactly why I usually tell people to focus and believe towards the process of meditation. That are a lot of different types of meditation available to us to exercise and also practice regularly. some of them might be in the form of some really complicated and hard to do type of yoga related things. But for the most part of it, it is really easy and can be done by anyone.

Anger management workbook for men

Whenever you are meditating they are a couple of things happening with you at the same time. The first thing that is going to be happening with you while you were meditating is that you are going to be putting a lot of your focus, To be honest, for the most part of it, onto a specific object or a specific thought inside your brain. When you were practicing on regular basis about putting your focus point up to a specific object for a certain amount of time you will be automatically giving your brain a healthy exercise for focus management. This will be able to clear your thoughts and also you will have a better perspective about the intersection that is happening around you. While that is being done, At the same time you will be also getting the proper expertise about how you can shift your focus on to the reasonable thing rather than just lashing out with anger regarding the situation that is happening at the moment. If you were practicing meditation on a regular basis then you will be able to put your focus on to anything that you like and also with full concentration. This will help you in terms of shifting your focus from your anger point towards something that is able to help you calm down. The next thing that happens with you whenever you are meditating is that you are going to be following a specific set of breathing techniques. And when you do that, You will be automatically training your body to consume a sufficient amount of oxygen that we are less likely to do on a regular basis. I know this is how to believe but this is actually the true. Whenever you are practicing to put your focus on to a certain topic for his other amount of time and also your practicing your breathing technique, you are going to be able to calm yourself down much faster and also your blood flow and your stream of thinking inside your brain is going to be much healthier and stable. You will have an increase amount of oil power and also concentration in terms of getting the results out of meditations.

Anger management workbook for men

That are also other things that will be happening with you whenever you are meditating. When you are putting your focus on to a certain point and also you have a stable rate of breathing you will automatically improve the blood flow onto your brain. And we all know that a healthy type of blood flow in our brain is obviously capable of making our thoughts much more clean.

Human beings are slave to one and one thing only. And that is the habit and the nature of them. If you're able to practice meditation for a certain amount of time each day or even a specific day of the week, you will automatically be starting to develop a sense of habit for doing it. And if you are doing it regularly then it is obvious that you are going to be having a sufficient and healthy blood flow in your brain and also you will be able to increase your concentration and will power up to a certain level.

There are some certain situations in which you might need the help of medicines. If you have visited any psychologist or psychiatrist, They might be able to give you a certain prescription regarding any medicine that will be able to come yourself down whenever you are at an angry state or about have any impulses. If you feel the necessity that you need to come yourself down on a quick business and you're not able to do it apart from any type of external help then you should probably speak first type of medical help. But even if you are seeking and taking such type of medical help you need to keep in your mind that the final result is you and yourself only. Because if you are getting too much dependent on those medicines it is very much possible that you will be nothing but a puppet of the medications.

Anger management workbook for men

I hope that I'm being able to explain to you the difference and the importance of both meditation and medication.

Medication is something that you should only keep yourself for the last resort. Even if you are taking any type of medicine sodium type of medical treatment for your anger management issues you should keep in your mind at all times that your main purpose is to get this entire thing under control by yourself. Doesn't matter what type of help or what type of support that you are getting from any type of exterior person, you always need to keep in your mind that you need to make yourself capable of handling the entire situation by yourself. That is your ultimate goal that you need to achieve at all costs. Anything else from that is only to be considered to you as an alternative that is temporary. The final objective of getting this entire thing solved and also managed in a specific way, is to make yourself capable and also change your prospective doors different type of emotions and responses towards impulsive situations.

With that being said, I am concluding this chapter. At the end of this book I will be giving you a brief summary about what you have learned so far and also I will be providing for the explanation for the things that I've said in this book. Let's have a little recap about what we have learned so far.

We have learned that the main thing behind changing your way about how much you are getting angry on a specific situation is to change your perspective. I'm not telling you that you should think every single little thing happening around you as positive things. I'm not telling you that you should not get married whenever you are saying someone else harassed or tortured in front of you. But whenever the situation is small and also you

Anger management workbook for men

know that's a step of circumstances are capable of making you angry then you need to change your perspective and think the other way around. The second most important thing that we have learned in this book is that at all costs you need to be keeping a pair of open eyes. Because despite of the situation might be quite obvious that the person in front of you is yelling at you for no reasons, there still might be a harsh reality for that person for which he has been acting irrationally.

I know that this doesn't justify the unfair behavior towards you done by the other person. But this might be able to help you think in a comfortable way and also it will be able to keep yourself calmed down.

The third important thing that we have learned about in this book is that we need to be putting proper attention towards the personal time and space. Because this is something that very less people actually think and do about. We need to give ourselves proper amount of time just to think about different circumstances and prospectives and also about the things that we have done and how things could have been better if we had taken an alternative step.

Anger management workbook for men

CHAPTER 13: EXTRAS

In this entire book I have told you several stories and also practical explanations about different things and different points that I have discussed. But one thing that is the most important among all of the points and all of the strategies that I have told you about anger management is that you need to be able to give yourself proper amount of time. I know that this might sound way too much childish and also a little bit lame to try by yourself. But if you can make yourself use to the habit of talking to yourself on a regular basis, it will be able to make yourself understand more and also open a lot of different perspectives about different situations. Because talking to ourselves is something that very less people do. But it is something that is required the most.

Let me tell you a little story about a friend that I know very closely before I finish this book. That person was quite well known in our class for being one of the most hot shot guy. Like literally, he was picking up fights with almost everyone at almost every single day. it was quite hard to find a single day or even a single period without him being getting into a fight. It was not like that he was a bully or that type of a person. But it was the situation that whenever someone has been doing something that he doesn't like or that really pisses him off he was getting triggered. After the certain amount of time the principal noticed about his behavior and also he did not think about it harshly. Which would have been the most common approach. But rather than just acting out of aggression towards him, The principal actually tried to understand behind the scenes reason of why he was

Anger management workbook for men

acting in such a way. After doing a little bit of research, our principal, Mr Daniels, found out that he had a lot of trouble in his home. He was a person that loves perfection in every single way. he loves a perfect set of table and chair along with the perfect arrangement of the books on top of it. He loves the perception of how the dishes are set on the table. He loves the perfection about how his entire room is managed and also how the house is totally neat and clean. But the thing is that, his mom and dad were both in the corporate sector. They were both lawyers working really long shifts in a law firm. That is why they had a little time to actually arrange their house in a proper manner. My friend, Justin, was having a really hard time in terms of adapting with the imbalances of the house. This is not something that is really bad or that is really criminal to happen in any home. But this is something that was really making him disturbed. That is why he was having a really short temper. Our principal knew that any type of traditional approach would do absolutely no good.

That is why he tried to talk to him personally. for days and days and months and months he used to visit Justin on a regular basis and also he tried to give as much as time as possible to just to talk to him and be there by his side as a person to whom Justin can talk to. We were quite shocked that just by the end of fall in that year, Justin was totally a different person that we knew.

This is what I've been trying to tell you all the time. If we are not giving ourselves proper time to talk about different things and also think about different things that has been disturbing us and also happening around us all the time, we will be not be able to come to any solution in terms of calming ourselves down.

You need to remember that doesn't matter what is happening and also doesn't matter what type of

Anger management workbook for men

approach you're taking towards making a proper angle management for yourself, your commitment and also how much positively you are able to think about it makes all the difference.

Anger management workbook for men

CONCLUSION

Listen, to be honest, anger management is not just something that someone can come and teach you right away. There is no specific prescription for this or any sort of specific guideline that you can follow.

As far as psychology goes, each individual person has his or her unique set of emotions and the way of reacting and handling them. The thing is that, no one can actually teach you to manage your anger. The thing that you can get in the form of help is the things and in the way that I have discussed the information with you.

There can only be some form of guide as to what to expect and which path to walk. The part of waling the path is totally on you.

Anger has done so many damages to so many people in countless ways. Apart from the personal life and the totally isolated anger issues, severe level of aggression and the level of world of violence that we see right now, is also a result of the failure of individual anger management.

You need to always remember that, anger is never good. It has never done good to anyone. Even it seems to be benefitting in some cases, please remind yourself that it does more damage than it does good to you.

I am not an expert psychiatrist or anything like that. I am just a normal person, here to help you out with one of the most suffered problems ever known by

Anger management workbook for men

mankind. The problem, that if there was a fixed solution to this, the world would be almost comparable to heaven right now.

You can also check out some of the other books that I have worked on. Most of them are for personal well-being and self-development.

And if you are a bit skeptical about spending more money on books like this, then I have that covered that for you as well. Most of my self-help or self-development books are available on amazon for totally free in the form of audio books. Even the intro is bound to make you interested to learn more and take better control of your life, that I can say boldly and confidently.

www.ingramcontent.com/pod-product-compliance
Lightning Source LLC
Chambersburg PA
CBHW072101110526
44590CB00018B/3268